Golf in the Wild

Going Home

397/1000

Golf in the Wild

Going Home

Robin J. Down

Illustrations by James A. Down

First published in the United Kingdom in 2022 by
northumbrian : light

Produced by the The Choir Press

ISBN 978-0-9928717-1-0

Contents

Acknowledgements

This sequel would never have been written but for the enthusiasm and support I received for the first book. Unlike the antagonistic world of social media, real-world people are generally civilised and kind, so the generous words from family, friends and the members of Allendale Golf Club, while much appreciated, might be simply attributed to politeness. The real test would come from the reaction of complete strangers. To name but a few who exhibited remarkable enthusiasm for *Golf in the Wild*: David Crossley, David and Patrick Shaw Stewart, Chris Morrison, Lucy Mackay, Tom Sampson, Tony Brown, Trevor Earthy, Gillean Ford, Mike Dutton, Jim Pendreigh, Julie Douglas, Roger and Kate Vincent and Gordon Chalmers. The unexpected joy of producing the first book has been that many of these once-strangers have become good friends and golfing buddies. The book has been a gateway to like-minded souls who share the same passions.

I must also mention Ali MacLeod, who enthusiastically helped with the section on Applecross in the first book. A virtual, online friend through his blog 'ApplecrossLife', we finally met at the Inn in 2015. He decided against being acknowledged and then regretted it. Tragically, Ali was drowned at sea while creel fishing from his boat, *Varuna*, in 2017.

Golf in the Wild: Going Home, once again, is far from just about golf, heading off in a wide divergent arc into history, the passing of time and the ghostly presences from my past. Local history research was much assisted by a host of good people who happily shared their time and knowledge as I progressed from Durness back to Allendale. In order of appearance in the book, I would like to express my sincere gratitude to the following: the MacKay family and The Strathnaver Museum, Bettyhill, Thurso for providing and granting permission to reproduce the images of Alec Mackay at Ard Neakie; Ronnie Lansley from durnesss.org for providing the Loch Eriboll U-boat image; Iain Morrison of the Melness Community Website, who provided much of the information relating to the sad story of Nik Wyper; Evan Sutherland, Reay Golf Club and Tom Stephen, whose knowledge of the course and local history proved invaluable; Gillean Ford for her continuing support and for providing the detail behind George Mackay's Titanic memorial at Skerray; Fergus Mather of The Wick Society Johnston Collection; Catherine McLeod, Wick Golf Club and Roy Mackenzie, the Wick Golf Club historian whose extensive knowledge and research helped shape the chapter devoted to Reiss Links; Bill Burns and Bill Glover of atlantic-cable.com whose Victorian undersea cabling expertise helped myself and Roy Mackenzie uncover the full history of the cable house at Reiss Links; Dr Victoria Connor, archivist and marketing assistant, The Carnegie Club, Skibo Castle; Lynne Mahoney, curator, HistoryLinks Museum, Dornoch; Terry Jones, Bonar Bridge, Ardgay Golf Club; Harry Corbett, Portmahomack Golf Club; Wing Commander Chris Barker RAF (retd), who provided the fascinating insight into flying the RAF SEPECAT Jaguar over Tarbat Ness; Trevor Robson and John Bowmaker of Beamish Golf Club, whose many conversations during our seniors' matches inspired the trip to Fortrose & Rosemarkie; Andy Burnett, designer and owner of Covesea golf course; Jean Watt, Cullen Golf Club; Mark Street, secretary of Carrbridge Golf Club; Nevin McGhee, archivist at the Glasgow Golf Club; Rose and Brian Thorburn of Black Bull Inn, Earlston, who provided a wealth of information relating to the Earlston Golf Club (and their moon course) and assisted with my Lauder enquiries; George Gilchrist of Newcastleton Golf Club; Ian 'L-Plate' Crocker, whose good company I enjoyed on the belated 'research' trips to Gifford, Anstruther and elsewhere throughout the writing of this sequel; long-term golfing buddy, Mike Metcalfe, whose calm and patient approach to the game and life has failed to rub off on me in almost twenty years; and finally, Malcolm Aitchison of Allendale Golf Club, who took the time to walk with me around the abandoned Thornley Gate course and made an imaginary round real.

I must also mention Tim Dickson and his excellent magazine, *Golf Quarterly*, which not only helped promote the first book but remains an entertaining source of fascinating and quirky golf stories.

Neither book would have been written but for the love of Allendale Golf Club which continues to flourish. Special mention must go to Neil Forsyth, our secretary and dedicated greenkeeper. Ably assisted by Ian Robinson, Neil has been instrumental in the club's recent renaissance. I should perhaps also credit Kevin Philipson and Neil with their wayward experiences of playing Portmahomack and Carrbridge.

I must also acknowledge the artistic prowess of 'our James' who has once again provided a fine set of illustrations to accompany each chapter heading. He is the only real artist in the family.

Finally, this journey, and all the ones to follow, begin and end with 'my trouble', the Good Wife:

> *There will come a time when*
> *You and I are invisible,*
> *To all but you and me.*
> *And I'll sing each line*
> *That appears with the years,*
> *'Till there's countless rings on our proud old tree.*
> *And I'll always get hold of you.*
> *My heart at the double.*[1]

---

1   'My Trouble' from Elbow's eighth studio album, *Giants of All Sizes*. Both books have been written to a soundtrack predominated by this band. I am sure Guy Garvey would not countenance golf, but Craig Potter, the band's keyboard player, is an enthusiastic amateur.

Introduction

Golf in the Wild: Going Home has been an entirely different undertaking compared to the first book. Setting off on that initial adventure, I knew from the outset where I was heading and how to get there. In this sequel, I knew the beginning and the end, but how they would join up was a journey into the unknown. It was also a journey I felt compelled to take—there would have been a strong sense of a 'job left undone' if I had not *gone home*.

The parameters for choosing golfing destinations changed through necessity. The first book visited only 9-hole courses, mostly with honesty boxes. Travelling across the top of Scotland, you would journey great distances before encountering anywhere that satisfied these criteria. Consequently, the first two courses visited are eighteen holes, but none the worse for that. Reay and Reiss Links more than satisfy all other aspects of the *Golf in the Wild* criteria—wonderful courses in spectacular locations, with beautifully presented and, generally, empty fairways.

At Lybster and Bonar Bridge I return to more familiar 9-hole territory, but in so doing, I inevitably miss out numerous beautiful courses, some of the best in Scotland. Omission does not imply disapproval; they simply do not fit the criteria, the narrative and/or the journey. Perhaps the only exception would be Helmsdale, which on both occasions I visited was sadly neglected. Their Facebook pages now suggest a revival. If this is correct, a visit would be recommended, as the setting on the banks of that fine salmon river, the Helmsdale, has the potential to be a delight.

After Bonar Bridge, Portmahomack on the Tarbat Ness peninsula was an entirely logical and delightful destination for golf and much else. A fine links-style course in the heart of the community, I would rush back there in an instant. To avoid retracing my steps, I headed directly south to Nigg, passing by a series of abandoned courses which only serve to remind how extensive was golf-mania at the turn of the nineteenth century. Harry Ward's *Forgotten Greens* is an excellent companion on such journeys, if occasionally melancholic, serving to remind how much has been lost. Travelling between a series of *Golf in the Wild* courses in the early 1900s would have been a much easier endeavour than now.

The journey from Nigg to the Black Isle is dependent on a ferry service that only runs in the summer, and given low traffic volumes, may not survive in the long term—beware. Crossing to Cromarty. It is here that *Golf in the Wild* really deviates from the desire to find 9-hole tracts in out-of-the-way places. Fortrose & Rosemarkie is a magnificent links course in a fine setting; but not only is it the full eighteen, but it will be busy in the summer months. I pitched up late in the day, and the pro kindly treated me to a twilight rate. Standing alone on the first at a big course you have never played can also be intimidating. The golf progressed pleasingly on the front nine as I joined up with a friendly local. The back nine? Well, that is another story. You will have to read on.

If Traigh was my favourite course in the first book, then Covesea is the best in the sequel. I have played it several times, and the experience is never a disappointment. Andy Burnett has created something special which deserves recognition at least on a par with the nearby Moray courses. A magnificently imagined layout created in recent times, it is followed by the equally imaginative Cullen Links. Another 18-hole links played on two levels, it may be short with ten par 3s, but this is a unique test of golf over and around an ancient rocky landscape.

From Cullen, south, I return to a series of 9-hole courses before arriving back at Allendale. It was south of Blair Atholl that COVID-19 struck and the options for visiting courses in Scotland became severely curtailed. The route taken is much as intended, the primary exclusions being Anstruther and Gifford. All I can do is recommend these as detours should anyone decide to follow in the path of *Golf in the Wild: Going Home.* The par 3 loop at the southern end of Anstruther is a particular delight. Everyone should experience the fifth, *The Rockies*, deemed the toughest par 3 in Britain in 2007 by *Today's Golfer*. Further south, Gifford is such a well-presented course, I would put it on a par with Carrbridge (see Chapter 10).

An unexpected consequence of exposing my mother-son relationship in the first book is that she developed a small fan club with requests for more of her exploits in the sequel. I have obliged with a degree of reluctance. It was never my intention to elevate Peg to stardom; indeed, I am slightly piqued by this development. Also making guest appearances are my Aunt Bet, Uncle Ed and cousin Brian. As my parents were both only children, I must explain.

The story is that my mum found Bet wandering the streets of Chorlton, Manchester, in a severely distressed state. The previous night, her house had been destroyed by the Luftwaffe. Homeless, with no nearby relatives, my mum, who was expecting my sister, took these strangers in, and so began a lifelong friendship. When I eventually appeared, I had a ready-made aunt and uncle. Bet was not immune to my mother's foibles, but she never forgot her kindness: "Your mum has a heart of gold."

Growing up in the 1950s, the war was a distant event from long ago, but for my parents, my aunt and my uncle, it was all recent history, the memories still fresh. For years, the families holidayed together, but Cullen in 1959 was the last of them, and for me the end of a happy era—I loved my Aunt Bet more than my mum. She was a soft and warm place to hide when Peg's heart lost its shine, as it frequently did.

When my mother was angry with me, which was often, she said, "The Devil led us to the wrong crib."[1] My mother never said this, but she would recognise the sentiment.

---

1   The opening lines of Jeanette Winterson's *Why Be Happy When You Could Be Normal?* I have also borrowed the closing line from this book.

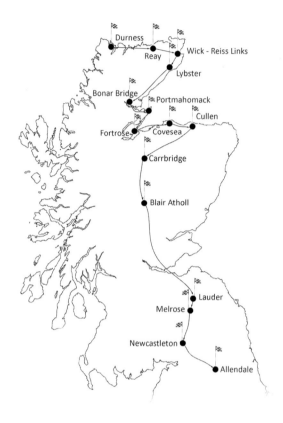

Durness–Reay: 61 miles
Reay–Reiss Links, Wick: 41 miles
Reiss Links, Wick–Lybster: 17 miles
Lybster–Bonar Bridge: 60 miles
Bonar Bridge–Portmahomack: 25 miles
Portmahomack–Fortrose: 42 miles (less if the Nigg–Cromarty ferry is operating)
Fortrose–Covesea: 51 miles
Covesea–Cullen: 28 miles
Cullen–Carrbridge: 56 miles
Carrbridge–Blair Atholl: 56 miles
Blair Atholl–Lauder: 108 miles
Lauder–Melrose: 11 miles
Melrose–Newcastleton: 40 miles
Newcastleton–Allendale: 40 miles

Approximately 636 inspiring miles

The Road East

She said,
I know what it's like to be dead,
I know what it is to be sad.
Lennon–McCartney[1]

E lizabeth Sparkes is buried in the small graveyard at Balnakeil, but I cannot find her. Somewhere, she is lying among the old stones, eternally listening to the sea. She is so far from home and days from her sisters: Mary, Anne, Julia and Harriet. She has no hope of escape, eternally at rest in bad company.

In the same graveyard, Donald McMurdo is easier to find; his tomb is immediately visible, built into a niche in the south wall. A serial murderer and henchman for Clan Mackay, his speciality was to throw his victims down the blowhole at nearby Smoo Cave.

Such was his reputation, that the local clergy would not countenance his burial at Balnakeil but were persuaded, by a compromise and maybe the greasing of palms, to bury him half in and half out of the sacred ground. The result is that his memory is better preserved than those of the good souls that surround him. He would no doubt have been proud of his epitaph: *Donald McMurdo here lies low - Was ill to his friend, and worse to his foe.*

The road leading down from the car park at Durness golf course squeezes between the graveyard and the sea and leads the traveller east. The final chapter of the first volume of *Golf in the Wild* ends with these words: *There is an echo of polite applause on a gentle wind rising across the Parph. I pick my ball from the hole, replace the pin and we go our separate ways. I am done.*

Except, I am not. In a literary sense, I have been stranded at Durness since *Golf in the Wild* was first published in August 2014. Like Elizabeth, I am alone in the land of the Vikings with no direction home. Unlike Elizabeth, I can move on. It is time to head east. It is time to head for Reay.

The road back to the village of Durness passes Balnakeil Craft Village before reaching the junction with the A838. The route home to Allendale Golf Club will head east along Scotland's northernmost shore before heading south again. The A838 loops inland at Sangomore before returning to the coast and cresting the hill next to Durness Village Hall. To the right of the hall's entrance is the John Lennon Memorial Garden. From the age of nine to fourteen, Lennon travelled to Sutherland for his summer holidays, and the story is that when he wrote these words, he was in part remembering his time at Durness:

There are places I remember all my life.
All these places had their meanings with lovers and friends.
In my life I've loved them all.[2]

Inscribed on three separate standing stones, they form the centrepiece of the memorial.

His connection with Durness was established through Elizabeth Sparkes, 'Mater', one of his maternal aunts, and one of the five Stanley girls—Harriet, Anne, 'Seashell Eyes'[3] Julia, his mother and Mary, known as 'Mimi'—with whom Lennon spent much of his childhood. Following the death of her first husband, Elizabeth remarried an Edinburgh dentist, Bertie Sutherland, who owned a croft in nearby Sangomore, and so Lennon's connection with the area began. The memories of holidays with his cousin Stan and the love of the area never dimmed.

Lennon's upbringing and the impact on his personality is well documented: the deserting father, Julia's wayward and uninhibited personality, his care being handed over to Aunt Mimi from a young age and the tragic road accident that killed Julia in July 1958, run over by an off-duty policeman. These were family events and tragedies that would assume significance far beyond the confines of the immediate Stanley family. A host of minor characters had walk-on parts, all with their exits and entrances.

One such player with a walk-on part was Nigel Walley, a junior golf professional from Liverpool's Lee Park Golf Club. Moments before Julia's accident, she had been talking and joking with John's childhood pal, Nigel. A short time after they went their separate ways on Menlove Avenue, Julia was run down by Eric Clague in his Standard Vanguard. In the immediate aftermath John would not speak to Nigel, holding him indirectly responsible for not delaying Julia for a few more crucial moments. At some point John and Nigel were reconciled, and for a brief period Nigel would manage The Quarrymen, Lennon and McCartney's forerunner to The Beatles. It was Nigel who organised a performance at Lee Park Golf Club, which proved to be an audition for a first appearance at the Cavern Club on 7 August 1957. Dr Joseph Sytner was a member at Lee Park and his son, Alan, was the founder and owner of the Cavern Club. Eight years later, on 15 August 1965, The Beatles appeared at Shea Stadium, New York City, in front of 55,600 hysterical fans. The tempestuous journey, from local golf club to the home of the New York Mets, is such stuff as dreams are made of.

The A838 keeps near company with the coast east of the village hall before diving south near Rispond, along the sinister shore of Loch Eriboll. A mile south, a turning to the left takes you down to Portnacon, where the Heilam Ferry once provided a passenger service to Ard Neakie, a would-be island on Eriboll's eastern shore, attached to the mainland by a narrow strip of sand and shingle. The ferry used to shortcut the 11-mile hike around the southern reaches of the loch.

Viewed from above, on the main road, Ard Neakie appears a bleak place, the main evidence of earlier human endeavour being the lime kilns. I passed by this abandoned settlement in another life, and so I am compelled to stop, exploring the lives of others while reliving my own. It was not always so desolate.

The kilns processed limestone quarried from the high ground of Ard Neakie and from Eilean Choraidh, an island in the middle of

Loch Eriboll. The quarry workers' lodgings were on the northern side of the approach to the imposing nineteenth-century ferry house. The ferry house was not only home to the ferryman and his family but was also a shop providing supplies to North Sea trawlers seeking shelter from a storm. With trawlermen, quarry workers, the shop, the ferryman and his passengers, the boats transferring limestone from Eilean Choraidh and the ships dispatching lime to east-coast farmers, on some days Ard Neakie bustled.

The history of this place, and Sutherland in general, is encapsulated in the lives of one family. Without these stories, Ard Neakie is just a collection of old stones and rotting timbers.

When Anne and her husband, Alexander Mackay,[4] were cleared from their croft at Totaig, they were resettled at Achnahuaigh, Melness, just south of Port Vasgo, at the head of the Kyle of Tongue. It was here they raised their daughter, Dolina, who would, in 1887, marry local cabinet maker, George Mackay. George had been planning to better himself by emigrating to Canada but was persuaded by the Duke of Sutherland to use his woodworking skills as a boatbuilder and to run the Heilam Ferry from Ard Neakie across Loch Eriboll to Portnacon. They raised seven sons at the ferry house, the eldest being Hugh, who would eventually qualify as a teacher, having studied at Aberdeen. Hugh's highway to Aberdeen was by sea, regularly catching a lift from trawlers as they stopped by at Ard Neakie. This connection with the sea is significant and points to a time when these coastal communities were better served by water than land.

Hugh served with the 1st Battalion Seaforth Highlanders during the Great War and survived, despite being declared 'missing, presumed dead'. He returned to teaching, married his first love,

Catherine Sutherland, and eventually retired to Connel Ferry, near Oban. Once he left home, he never lived again at the big house on Ard Neakie, unlike younger brother, Alec.

Alexander Mackay was born in 1889 and attended Eriboll School before joining his father, George, to run the ferry and to learn the trade of boatbuilding. Like my grandfather, Fred, Alec was in the Territorial Reserve, and both would see active service at Gallipoli. The Dardanelles land campaign was abandoned after eight months' fighting, and the invasion force was withdrawn to Egypt. Transferring from Alexandria, Alec would see service in Macedonia and France, whereas Fred transferred into the Royal Flying Corps (RFC) and served the rest of the war at the RFC Training School, Aboukir.

Alec survived the war but suffered disfiguring facial injuries in France and was not finally discharged until March 1920. The expectation was that Eriboll Farm would be divided to provide land for returning local servicemen, and Alec was fully expecting to receive a share. In another example of shoddy behaviour by the estates and landowners, this never happened, so Alec returned to boatbuilding and operating the Heilam Ferry with his father.

In this photograph of the young Alec, he is standing in front of the workers' lodgings holding a large salmon by the gills.[5]

A prize catch for an innocent young man dressed in heavy tweed. The man who returned to Ard Neakie was not the same boy who went to war in 1914. The demons that accompanied him as he walked back down the strand to the front door of the ferry house in 1920 can only be imagined.

He would live out the rest of his days on Ard Neakie, where he died a bachelor in 1957. *A million burning candles for the love that never came.*[6] (Leonard Cohen)

On the road to Reay, I returned to this abandoned place for the first time in thirty years. There are no 'keep out' signs, nor are there indications of rights of way. This is the homeland of the 'right to roam'. It was much as I remembered, except there is now no trace of the quarry workers' lodgings. The final approach sits between

7

shingle, north and south; the ferry house a design in symmetry; the pier still solid where no boats call; the lime kilns with their cavernous openings sensibly fenced; the convenient limestone quarry just a wheelbarrow's walk from the kiln tops; the climb higher still, such that Portnancon can be seen across the loch—the departure point for the Heilam Ferry.

The blue skies hosted mountainous nimbus clouds, and the sun shone intermittently, but there was a strong Arctic wind blowing in from the north. As I made to leave between the shores, a gust of wind opened the front door to the ferry house. It seemed like an invitation. Alec Mackay had summoned me into his family home. Exploring all three floors of the abandoned house, it was not the sound of the wind I heard blowing through the rafters and ill-fitting windows; it was the sound of distant voices and the rattle of Alec's Indian PowerPlus motorcycle combination.

This image is dated 1924.[5] The last of the family did not leave the ferry house until 1990. Since then the lease has not been renewed and the building remains empty, except for the echoes from the past. The kilns are cold, and the ferry no longer plies the waters across Eriboll, but the loch is not always silent.

Loch Eriboll is the deepest seawater loch on mainland Great Britain, offering sanctuary from the high seas around Cape Wrath. Consequently, it regularly plays host to a variety of large naval vessels. It was on these waters that the crew of HMS *Hood* spent their last shore leave before the ill-fated encounter with the German battleship *Bismarck* at the Battle of Denmark Strait in May 1941. Bizarrely, four years later, in May 1945, the Germans dropped anchor in the loch. What would Alexander Mackay have made of such an intrusion by this old enemy? In the space of twelve days, no fewer than thirty-three U-boats would surrender in these waters.

9

These were no yellow submarines, and there was no life of ease. They were not even proper submarines; *they were essentially diesel-powered surface ships which could travel submerged for short periods and at slow speed using electric power from their auxiliary engine.*[7] Recharging the electric motors on the surface would take eight hours at reduced speed and four if stationary and highly vulnerable. The most common craft, the Type VII, could accommodate a crew of forty-six; there were no washing facilities, no change of clothes and no fresh air circulation when submerged, and the submariners lived with constant damp. When the boats surfaced, the equalisation of pressure caused the water in the dank vessel to evaporate, and the boat filled with steam. Above and beneath the waves it was a fetid world of sweat, noise, marine oil and torrid temperatures. In supposed compensation, food was good quality, plentiful and stored in every spare nook and cranny throughout the boat—it all tasted of diesel. This was a gruesome place to die, and many did; between 1939 and 1945, 733 U-boats were lost. In return, they sank 2,753 Allied ships.

It is hard to imagine the reaction of the locals when the first submarines appeared. Did the armed forces keep them informed or did they expect them to open fire? Was this surrender or a last stand? What exactly were the intentions of the U-boat commanders? In the event, they simply used the loch as a dumping ground for munitions before being dispatched to tent camps in England. The U-boats were then scuttled in the Atlantic by the Royal Navy as part of Operation Deadlight.[8] This strange episode also has parallels with *Whisky Galore!* Among the surrendering U-boats, there was U-1231, which was used as the fleet's underwater off-licence—it was stock full of wine. It is not clear if this was thrown overboard or sold under the counter at the nearby Heilam Inn on the west bank of the loch, at Portnancon. Possibly, it stayed on board. This U-boat was eventually transferred to the Soviet Union as war booty and remained in service with the Baltic Fleet until the mid-1950s.

Emerging into the fresh light and sweet air of Loch Eriboll, there must have been an overwhelming sense of relief: relief that they had survived, relief that they could escape the stinking submersible coffins, relief that everything they ate would no longer be tinged with diesel and relief that it was all finally over.[9]

Climbing away from Eriboll and Ard Neakie, the road takes you on what J. Hubert Walker, writing in 1948, described as *one of the loneliest roads in the country*. T. Ratcliffe Barnett makes these observations in *Autumns in Skye, Ross and Sutherland*, written in 1930:

We were creeping up the road and round this rock at the top, when, like a bolt from the blue and without a sound, a

*motor-bicycle whisked round the rock, on the wrong side of
the road, scooted across the nose of the car and, by a
miracle, did not skid on the grass and so somersault down the
slope to the sea. But somebody ought to have been killed. All
which things I deliberately record to indicate that Sutherland
roads are very narrow, very rough, often dangerous, and that
only fools rush on where angels hold their breath.*

Perhaps it was an Indian.

T. Ratcliffe Barnett's words should have been recommended
reading for John Lennon. In 1969, in the space between The
Beatles' last live performance on top of the Apple HQ in Savile
Row and the start of the recording session that would become
the *Abbey Road* album, John Lennon and Yoko Ono made a road
trip to Scotland, taking with them their respective children,
Julian and Kyoko. It was a sentimental journey—the opportunity
to introduce a new-found love to the past that shaped him and
the places he remembered.

There have been improvements since 1930, but T. Ratcliffe
Barnett's observations remain valid, even more so in 1969.
Heading for Durness, Lennon, the short-sighted and
unenthusiastic motorist, drove his car off the road on the
single-track A838 somewhere between Tongue and Loch Eriboll.
Julian Lennon was the only one to escape unharmed, the other
three being transferred to the Lawson Memorial Hospital,
Golspie. It was only Julian who made it to Durness, where he
was collected by an irate Cynthia Lennon.

The video of the Apple HQ live performance looks contemporary,
despite being filmed nearly fifty years ago. The nonchalance, the

arrogance and the style are directly from the future, the twenty-first century. They could all pass for hipsters, only Starr's vinyl red coat jars. The anachronisms are parked in the London streets below—cars that are firmly rooted in the early part of the twentieth century.

Austin Drawing Office (ADO) 14 was the project code name for the Austin Maxi, one in a series of similar British Motor Corporation (BMC) vehicles vying for the unlovely awards. Another ugly duckling was the ADO17, the BMC 1800 variants, affectionately known as 'land crabs'. None of these cars achieved rock or cult status in their day, but the Maxi could lay claim to one unlikely pilot: it was a Maxi that Lennon drove off the A838. Following the accident, this white example of the ADO14 vehicle was taken back to Lennon's home at Tittenhurst Park, near Ascot, and mounted on a plinth to remind John and Yoko of the fragility of life and BMC products in general.

Heading further east, the A838 twists through a bleak terrain as Ben Loyal stands tall on the southern horizon. Cresting a rise, the Kyle of Tongue shimmers in the distance and announces a distinct change in landscape as the road approaches the 2.4-mile causeway, built in 1971 to replace a passenger ferry and a ten-mile detour by road around the head of the Kyle. To the left of the approach to the bridge and causeway is the road to Melness and Talmine.

I know this place. I remember the many days along the edges of the Kyle. I remember scrambling at low tide to the feathery eider nests on Talmine Island while nervous mothers sat tight; the night a pod of dolphins performed aquatic ballet in Tongue Bay, between Midtown and Scullomie; the dunes as high as water towers, with sand so soft you could run down their steep faces, safe in the arms of gravity; the day on Rabbit Islands in the company of seals and the nervous wait on the shore (would the fisherman remember us?); spinning off the rocks near the causeway as oystercatchers, in faithful pairs, skimmed the fast-running tide near inquisitive *selkies* (seals), heads bobbing in the water, watching our every move; the sad sight of the lone grebe, too exhausted to fly from its watery grave beneath Ard Skinid; the evening walks to the little that remained of Port Vasgo, and the abandoned boats along the shoreline at Talmine; the busy otter scurrying across the sands at low tide, beneath Tongue Lodge, late—so late—for a very important date; catching a first brown trout on Loch a' Mhuilinn—a fish so young, it knew no better than to rise to my inexpert fly; and always a harem of seals sunning on the sandbar. All of this and the reminder of how fragile we are: the beautifully sculpted, poignant headstone at Melness cemetery.

The young man had memories like mine and more. Hauling lobster pots from near Port Vasgo, he was washed into an unforgiving sea amid the dangerous undercurrents and deep water that twist between the inlets and Stac Dubh.

There is another memorial at the spot where it happened. *Sadly, the stone and the cairn are broken, like the hearts of his family. By all accounts he was a fine young lad who loved Melness, its beauty and its freedom.*[10]

IN

MEMORY OF

NIK WYPER

WHO WAS SWEPT

FROM THESE ROCKS

ON

29TH JUNE 1989

AGED 18 YEARS

A YOUNG MAN

WHO WILL ALWAYS

BE REMEMBERED

"GOING HOME"

The A838 crosses the causeway towards Tongue, loops around the Tongue Hotel and becomes the A836 before heading east above Tongue Bay. Eventually, the road crosses the River Borgie at Borgie Bridge, or more accurately Borgie Bridges—there are two, the old and the new. Further east the road is carried across the River Naver at Invernaver and climbs towards Bettyhill on the river's eastern flank. On the right sort of day, the Naver carries a bright white light down to the North Sea, running out into saltwater below beach and dune—perfect golfing terrain.

The road east from Bettyhill takes you through a series of clearance villages—Armadale, Strathy and Melvich—crossing the Halladale River and finally reaching Reay. The course and clubhouse are clearly visible from the main road. It is time to play some golf.

Notes

1. 'She Said, She Said' is attributed to Lennon-McCartney, but like many of their compositions, one or other was the primary songwriter. This was very much a John Lennon creation, to the extent that McCartney is understood not to have performed on the original 1966 *Revolver* recording.

2. 'In My Life' is another Lennon–McCartney composition which is almost entirely attributable to Lennon. 'He called 'In my Life' his first 'real, major piece of work. Up until then, it had all been glib and throwaway.' (*John Lennon: In his Own Words* by Ken Lawrence). The three individual lines are etched into three separate granite slabs at the heart of the memorial garden.

3. From the lyrics of 'Julia', written for his mother (1914–1958). It is the final song from '*The White Album*'. A second song about Julia, 'Mother', was recorded in 1970 and appeared on the *John Lennon/Plastic Ono Band* album. It contains these telling lines: *Mamma, don't go. Daddy, come home.*

4. This is the land of the Mackays. According to houseofnames.com, *the chronicle of the name Mackay begins with a family in the Pictish clans of ancient Scotland. The name is derived from the personal name Aodh, a cognate of Hugh. The Gaelic form of the name is usually Mac Aoidh, and in Inverness the Gaelic form of the name Mackay is Mac Ai.*

5. The images of Alec Mackay are reproduced with the kind permission of the Mackay family and The Strathnaver Museum, Bettyhill, Thurso.

6. An extract from 'You Want It Darker', the title track from Leonard Cohen's fourteenth and last studio album, released on 21 October 2016—nineteen days before he died.

7. A quote from Bob Carruthers' *Wolf Pack, The U-Boats at War* (*Hitler's War Machine)* from the Pen & Sword Maritime Books series.

8. Operation Deadlight was the code name for the Royal Navy operation which scuttled 116 of the 156 U-boats surrendered to the Allies at the end of the war.

9. The image of the U-boat surrender is reproduced with the kind permission of Durness.org: 'The Past and Present of Durness'. The image was donated to Durness local archive by Mr Billy Morrison, now deceased. He was given the photograph by a professional news photographer after the war.

10. An extract from correspondence with Iain Morrison of the Melness Community Website, who provided much of the information about young Nik Wyper. The subtitle for this book was chosen long before any knowledge of the memorial at Stac Dubh. Both refer to Mark Knopfler's 1983 *Going Home: Theme of the Local Hero*, the soundtrack to David Puttnam's film, *Local Hero*.

Reay

And the crescent sands like a golden band, still enclasps the sapphire bay.
Robert S. Stephen[1]

T here is a wild beauty to this place which is quite different from the west. After the high uplands of Sutherland, Caithness is a gentler, flatter and a largely treeless landscape, where landmarks stand out like exclamation marks on the horizon. The golf course at Reay (pronounced Ray) owes its existence and survival to the occupants of Sandside House to the west and the Dounreay atomic energy site to the east. Both are visible from various parts of the course.

Thomas Pilkington, the St Helens glass manufacturer, acquired Sandside House and some of the surrounding estates in the late 1800s for use as a shooting and fishing retreat. Like many landed families of the nineteenth century, the Pilkington clan, relatives,

Chapter 2

friends and accompanying servants would up sticks from smoky Lancashire and spend the summer sporting in the far north. The contrast between industrialised St Helens and the wilds of Reay could not have been more pronounced. When not shooting, contemplating salmon or installing an early version of double glazing, Thomas's thoughts turned to golf. Looking east from the upper, condensation-free windows of Sandside House, he would see the perfect location for his very own course.

The links land between the dunes of Sandside Bay and the road to Thurso would be ideal for wielding a brassie, spoon, mashie and niblick. Bordered by Sandside Burn to the west, the Burn of Isauld to the east and with Reay Burn crossing its centre, this is ideal golfing terrain, offering scope for drainage and hazard alike. On 27 December 1893 a meeting was held at the Reay Inn to establish the golf club. The course would be maintained by the Pilkington family, and Thomas was duly elected as president. Access to the course was effectively shared between the Pilkingtons and the members of the club. The cricket-style pavilion, erected in 1899, reflects this division. One half was made available to the Pilkington family and guests, while the other was occupied by the club members. One place for the gentry; one place for the hoi polloi.

By 1895 the club was organising friendly matches with nearby Wick, established in 1870. The *John O'Groat Journal* of 28 June 1895 filed this report, a sporting commentary firmly rooted in the nineteenth century:

It is a splendid natural course, planned out in twelve holes by a professional who knew his business. The bunkers, burns and other obstacles are not artificial. They were laid down at the creation in a way that marks out the place as one intended for the great game of golf, although only put to the use for which it was intended within the past few years.

There is already in Reay a joiner who can make a wooden club that will play, and play well. When the amount of bad clubs and blasphemy that enter into the great game of golf are taken into

account, should not a laurel wreath be awarded to the man who can make a wooden club that will calm the troubled spirit of the golfer and promote peace and good will among men?

The modern-day course is the most northerly 18-hole links course on the British mainland. It starts and ends with a par 3, *Beinn Ratha*, and this first hole is a tough opener. At 235 yards, hitting the green in regulation is no mean achievement. The course record of 63 was set by Don Mackay on 15 May 2004, starting with a bogey 4 at the first. I matched his score here, but nowhere else. The second, *Sandside*, a par 4 with out-of-bounds along the left, heads north-west, reaching the second green after 428 yards. This is roughly the location of the original clubhouse, with access from the road to Fresgoe, which runs down to Sandside Harbour. This safe haven was built in 1830 by Major William Innes for both trade and fishing. The good major was an occupant of Sandside House prior to the Pilkingtons.

Loch an Eoin, the third, an easier 369-yard par 4, takes you back towards the clubhouse, and then the fun really begins. The fourth, *Sahara*, is a 581-yard par 5, ranked at stroke index 3. Flying the dunes in front of the tee, a solid drive is required to have any chance of seeing the eventual target with your second. On my first visit I optimistically headed for the nearest flag on the horizon, which turned out to be the fifth green, some 170 yards short of the intended destination. In a fit of frustration, I caught my third shot so sweetly, that it flew the green and headed towards Sandside Burn, never to be seen again. I guess it is now out at sea or buried on Sandside Beach, waiting for Alice Roberts' great-grand-daughter to excitedly dig it up 100 years hence. There will be many to choose from.

Apart from the pot bunkers, the relatively straightforward 144-yard par 3, the fifth, *Cnocstanger*, comes as welcome and light relief before the glorious sixth. Named *Braid's Choice*, it pays homage to the great golfer and course designer who was invited to the club in early 1933 in order to make recommendations for improvements to the 12-hole course and its potential expansion to eighteen holes. He was accompanied by the then vice-captain, John Carmichael, one of four sons to the Reverend Dugald Carmichael and his wife, Agnes, of Reay Manse. The proposed acquisition of land and the changes to the existing course were sadly beyond the means of a small club with limited finances, but it was not an entirely wasted endeavour. John Carmichael and his younger brother, Donald, had much to do with the reinstatement of the course in the late 1950s and early 1960s, and it seems almost certain that some of Braid's original suggestions took root in the new course. This is most obvious at the sixth and seventh, the original second and third, where Braid's suggestions have been followed to the letter.

James Braid is sometimes considered the man who refined the art of the dog-leg, and the sixth (originally the second) is a hole he singled out for commendation. He suggested moving the tee back and placing the green on the edge of the bank of the burn, while retaining the dog-leg. This is exactly how this hole is now presented—a perfect links par 5.

The layout of the original 12-hole course was quite different from its modern counterpart, although occupying much the same acreage. As you play the third through sixth holes, you are treading ground once occupied by the first, second, eleventh and twelfth—ground walked by Thomas Pilkington and the club captains, of which there were just five between 1893 and 1940.

The year his father died, 1930, Alan Pilkington was elected captain and remained in post until 1940 and the demise of the old course. At the same time, responsibility for maintaining and running the course passed from the Pilkington family to the members, and in 1932 Alan would sell Sandside House. The outbreak of war signalled the end of the club and abandoning of the links to nature. While the start of hostilities marked an end to golf, it also gave rise to new beginnings and new opportunities. A few miles down the road the foundations of something entirely different were being laid.

When I was small and Christmas trees were tall[2] I was easily spooked by big things. Taken to the local fire station by my grandfather, I was reduced to tears by the sheer enormity of the engines. Given the opportunity to climb Portland Bill Lighthouse, the endless stairs sent me scurrying outside. The railway viaduct between Peover and Goostrey, in Cheshire, towered so high, I would not go near. In the fields nearby, an enormous and strange structure was taking shape, and I took exception to it. In the 1950s Bernard Lovell's radio telescope at Jodrell Bank was only partially complete.

Many years later, living in the foothills of the Peak District at Bosley, on clear days the entire Cheshire Plain was visible from the bedroom window. And there, at its centre, stood the Jodrell Bank Telescope. No longer something to be feared and no longer a stranger in the landscape, it had come to define it.

Around the same time in the 1950s, many miles further north, another strange structure was emerging from the white heat of technology.

At the outbreak of the Second World War, it became apparent that the air defences in the far north of Scotland must be improved because the British Navy's safe anchorage at Scapa Flow was particularly vulnerable to air attack. As a first step an airfield was constructed at Wick, and then, later in the war, another at Dounreay. However, the Dounreay facility, not completed until April 1944, was immediately mothballed. Apart from occasional usage by the Royal Navy as HMS Tern II and later as a camp for displaced Polish servicemen, it remained unused until 1954, when the government announced that Dounreay was to become the centre for UK fast reactor research and development. Between 1955 and 1958, the Dounreay Fast Reactor (DFR) sphere mushroomed into the landscape and, like Jodrell Bank, has come to define it. Lovell's creation exclaims, *Here we can reach for the stars.* Dounreay's says, *Here we can tinker with the tools of Armageddon and tame Einstein's monster.*

The DFR achieved criticality in 1959, and in 1962 it became the first fast reactor in the world to supply electricity to a national grid. Just fifteen years later it was switched off. Since then it has been a long slow process of decommissioning, an exercise that will not be complete until 2025, with the demolition of the sphere. Sadly, retention is not practical. According to the Dounreay Heritage Strategy Document, 2010, SES(09)P007, Issue 2:

> *The DFR sphere is contaminated throughout, and recent core samples from the vault indicate that the concrete has deteriorated more than anticipated and that original construction techniques may have been lax in some areas ... despite the most rigorous decontamination efforts, the risk of receiving a significant radiation dose may never go away.*

I have some connection with the Dounreay site, having been responsible for establishing a computer field trial there between 1988 and 1989. The main system was housed in the buildings adjacent to the DFR. It was an exercise I enthusiastically promoted, which had more to do with my love of travel and wild landscapes than the practicalities of running a software trial in this faraway place. It was during one of many site visits that I was given access to the sphere, much smaller on the inside than it appears from without. Fortunately, I had grown more tolerant of 'big things' in the intervening years. Now it is the things I cannot see that worry me, rather than the things I can.

At the seventh, the original third, Braid made more proposals that have found life in the new course. It is much like the original third, except the tee is moved further right to higher ground, bringing the pin into full view—exactly what was asked for by Braid. Now named *Pilkington*, in honour of the course's founder, it is a par 3, originally known as *Funker's Bunker*. The signature hole, it is remarkably testing and, frankly, beyond my golfing abilities. The green sits on an elevated plateau some 190 yards from the similarly elevated tee. To carry that distance, I need a wood, and the ball flight I achieve with such clubs is such that I may reach the green, but it would be a fleeting acquaintance, as the ball scurries through the green and buries itself in the rough beyond. Of course, I tried and inevitably found myself searching for the ball in the bankside. I guess it is best to play it as a par 4, lay up well short and hope for a good chip onto the green, not forgetting that Reay Burn comes into play and the options for bailing out are limited. It is challenging and, for one reason or another, memorable. As I frequently remind myself, golf is fundamentally a masochistic

endeavour. The photograph[3] shows the view from the back of the green, looking back to the tee. The hole is so notorious, it has even inspired verse.

> *There was a young man of Sandside,*
> *Who viewed Funker's Bunker with pride.*
> *As he drove from the tee,*
> *Said he'd do it in three,*
> *But he hadn't holed out when he died![4]*

Following the trials at *Pilkington*, the par 4 eighth, *Machar* is a welcome contrast as it heads north-east towards the east end of the course. This is immediately followed by the delightful 176-yard par 3 ninth, *Chapel*. The green is finely positioned with views west along the length of Sandside Bay. In this distant and remote land, the beaches are Cinerama wide and post-apocalyptic empty—not a whisper of shrieking children or barking dogs. Something more sinister than ball games is happening on these shores. Reay golf course overlooks Sandside Beach and is visible in all its glory in

the photograph above. Look closely, and there are two dots on the sand. The one on the left is a Land Rover, the support vehicle for the one on the right—the Groundhog—scouring the beach for radioactive particles.

An article published in the *New Scientist* in June 1995 explains:

Lid Blown Off Dounreay's Lethal Secret

by Rob Edwards

Early in the morning of Tuesday 10 May 1977 there was a loud explosion at the Dounreay nuclear plant on the north coast of Scotland. The UK Atomic Energy Authority, which runs the plant, had dumped at least 2 kilograms of sodium and potassium down a 65-metre shaft packed with radioactive waste and flooded with seawater.

The results were dramatic. The sodium and potassium reacted violently with the water. The explosion blew off the

27

shaft's huge concrete lid, threw its steel top plate 12 metres to one side, badly damaged the 5-tonne concrete blocks at the mouth of the shaft and blasted scaffold poles up to 40 metres away.

An eyewitness reported a plume of white smoke blowing out to sea. And, as government watchdogs revealed for the first time last week, the ground around the shaft was littered with radioactive particles hot enough to injure and kill. Over the past eighteen years, almost 150 such particles have been found on Dounreay's beaches.

I achieved something similar by poking bits of sodium down the plughole in the school chemistry lab. You would have thought someone in authority might have had a similarly 'inquisitive' education. The hit-and-miss clean-up will continue indefinitely.

While some might consider an atomic research establishment to be a less than ideal neighbour, it was the presence of the UK Atomic Energy Authority (UKAEA) that proved to be a lifesaver for the golf club. Aerial photographs of Reay, taken in the 1950s, show a course overwhelmed by the shifting sands of the dunes. It was the Taylor family, who took over the Sandside Estate after the Pilkingtons, who suggested that the Dounreay Sports and Social Club might like to lease the Sandside links and resurrect the golf club. Starting as a 9-hole course, similar to the original layout, it enlarged to fourteen holes, and then, in the 1960s, developed into the independent 18-hole club of today, complete with its own nineteenth hole, opened in 1964 and extended in the 1970s. The estate and local minister even granted permission for golf on Sunday, something King James VI had granted to the general populace in 1618.

The election of officers to the reconstituted club in May 1962 has a perfect historical symmetry. The new president would be Alan Pilkington, whose father was responsible for establishing the original 12-hole links course. Mrs Hilda Taylor, the wife of Captain Simon Taylor and owner of Sandside House, whose approaches to UKAEA resulted in the re-establishment of the course in the 1950s, was elected vice president. Finally, Donald Carmichael was confirmed as captain. Donald, raised in Reay, was a junior member of the original course up to its demise in 1940. By a strange quirk of circumstance, he was also the first permanent Atomic Energy Authority employee at Dounreay. An Edinburgh University philosophy graduate, he returned to Caithness during the Second World War to take charge of the northern radar stations. Following the war he was employed by the Ministry of Works, from where he was seconded to the Atomic Energy Authority Industrial Group, a forerunner of the UKAEA. Remarkably, he was responsible for negotiating the land deals at Isauld and Lower Dounreay that enabled the government to commence construction of its fast breeder reactor.

At the turn, the par 4 tenth, *Isauld*, heads 351 yards south across the top of the course, towards a green adjacent to Mary's Cottage. The fairway climbs towards higher ground, and if there is a prevailing cross wind, landing on, or even near, the green may prove a difficult second shot.

From this part of the course, the domed top of the DFR is clearly visible on the eastern horizon. A series of par 4s—*Torran*, *Chimneys* and *Spring Lochy*—take you down towards Reay Burn and back again. These are followed by another splendid par 5, *Mary's Cottage*, which climbs to the highest corner of the course—a testing three shots to the south side of the estate buildings. Making par on this uphill stroke index 4 hole is a fine achievement. In immediate contrast, the easiest hole on the course, the par 3 fifteenth, *Vikings Grave*, at 136 yards, should restore some equilibrium if the fourteenth was found to be tough going; you just need to avoid its three bunkers. While other parts of the course have been walked by early golfers, the terrain around the fifteenth has been trodden by much older soles— the clue is in the name. Examine the local OS map, and there are references to hut circles and standing stones in the near vicinity.

It was here, in 1926, that Viking remains were discovered. The location was described as *behind the drill hall*, a space now occupied by the garage, some 150 yards from the fifteenth fairway.

According to the National Record of the Historic Environment, *a male skeleton, complete from the knees upwards, was found among the sand dunes, not far from the north side of the drill hall at Reay. It lay full length on a paved surface, with the head slightly raised on a flat stone and was surrounded and covered by large stones and sand.*

I have no emotional attachment to Viking graves, but I am old enough to remember drill halls. They came into being following the formation of the Rifle Volunteer Corps in 1859. The composition of the volunteer forces would change over time, but the necessity for indoor training facilities was common to all reserves, and drill halls became a common feature of many towns and villages across the UK. When not in use for training, they were a convenient community asset, hosting meetings, dances and night classes. At Reay, the drill hall hosted the inaugural meeting of the reconstituted Reay Golf Club in May 1962.

I was raised in Hale, Cheshire—a place nothing like Reay, but it also boasted its own drill hall. A substantial building with a large, sunburst, round top window, it was a commanding presence in this dormitory town. It was built in 1876 as a roller-skating rink, at the height of 'rinkomania'. This craze arose from American, James Leonard Plimpton's, 1863 invention—a four-wheeled roller skate that could turn corners. It was a short-lived phenomenon, with the Hale rink closing after just three years. By 1888 it had become home to the Cheshire Volunteers and would remain a community asset until 1972, when it and the equally magnificent district council offices next door were demolished to make way for a hotel and supermarket.

Unlike Reay, the Hale Drill Hall did not succumb to a declining population; it was the victim of architectural vandalism. In 2015, when Trafford Council reviewed the Hale Station Conservation Area, the hotel and supermarket were considered *out of character with its surrounding environment, and even when considered as a standalone structure, it holds little architectural merit*.

This eyesore overlooks the bowling green and the remarkable monkey puzzle tree which has now grown out of all proportion to its surroundings.

Further along the road, level-crossing gates were once operated by a ship's wheel in the adjacent signal box. They have been replaced by continental barriers. These jar as much as the hotel and supermarket. Beyond the railway, Hale Cinema opened in 1923 and was demolished in 1979. This is a cherished place where never-forgotten little Susan introduced a bemused young boy to the delights of French kissing. In the smoke-filled darkness, on the back row, two pink tickets for a string of films we never watched.

Further still, the Burrows School of Dancing—another place to meet girls. I had no interest in dancing, unlike my big sister who preceded me. Musically from a different age, her record collection was comprised of Del Shannon, Pat Boone, Buddy Holly, Bobby Vee and Neil Sedaka; nothing so succinctly defined our age gap as our taste in music. A star on the dance floor, she won badges and prizes and was once pictured in the *Altrincham, Hale and Bowdon Guardian*—a low-level photograph of a twirling jive skirt. Too much was revealed for my mother. "I did not carry you through the Blitz so you could show your knickers to the world."

> *Come dancing,*
> *That's how they did it when I was just a kid.*
> *And when they said come dancing,*
> *My sister always did.*[5]

At faraway Reay, the drill hall was replaced by a garage, people bought cars and the slow decline of village life began. Drive through Reay, and many other similar-sized communities today, and they seem deserted, but this was not always the case. Up to the mid twentieth century and beyond, people regularly walked to the local shops for groceries and morning and evening would pop out for newspapers, the only source of in-depth news. People left their house for distraction, going to the local inn or any number of events at the village hall. By necessity, they walked far more. Rural agricultural labourers, of which there were many, would walk great distances for work.

The car, TV, supermarkets and the Internet have conspired to turn us into insular beings. The streets are empty, and something has been lost.

When the shops, pubs and village halls disappear from these remote places, a local golf club in the wild can provide the twin virtues of sociability and exercise.

And so to the finishing holes; the sixteenth, a downhill, 314-yard par 4, *Reay Kirk*, is the final descent towards Reay Burn and provides the opportunity to stand and stare at a glorious panorama. Out-of-bounds threatens all the way down the left, and I duly pulled my drive, narrowly avoiding disaster. I was able to find my ball, inches from a white stake, which only serves to highlight that I was playing the course in April, when the rough was at its thinnest and the wind was not blowing. Frankly, the conditions flattered my golf. I can imagine this being a real test when the westerlies are at their strongest. The locals must be used to this. Perhaps, like the Muirfield man, *on calm days he finds it difficult to maintain his balance, for lack of something to lean against.*[6]

The par 4 seventeeth, *Dossie's Dyke*, may be relatively short, but with a burn to cross—a narrow approach and punishing rough left and right—there is scope to undo much of the good work of the previous holes.

In 2006 Reay Golf Club won the BIGGA[7] Golf Environment Award, and in recognition produced a highly informative guide to the environmental and conservation management of the course. It is a fascinating read which adds another dimension to playing the course. Describing the seventeenth, it states that *wildlife may not always be obvious*, *particularly on a cold and windy day*, *as it prefers to stay hidden and out of harm's way. Subtle clues, such as fox scat or owl pellet, within these grasslands, throughout the seventeenth hole, provide evidence of a diverse and interesting nightlife.* So when you find yourself tramping around in the rough, looking for that lost Titleist, take a closer look at the undergrowth.

The round finishes as it starts—with a par 3. Unlike the first, the eighteenth, *Clachan*, is a friendly, straightforward 162-yard drive back to the clubhouse, assuming you can avoid the deep pot bunkers left and right. On the horizon, the tops of the graveyard memorials watch like a thinning crowd at the end of a long day at the Open. These silent spectators brought the best out in me, and I duly parred the last, always good for leaving a favourable impression of a golf round. Par or not, this is a thoroughly enjoyable true links course. In the words of Donald Steel, the course architect and former golfer, "In a different location, it would enjoy worldwide acclaim." Fortunately, its inaccessibility should ensure that golf in this wild place will remain an unhurried and solitary experience.

Notes

1. An extract from 'Sunset Soliloquy' by local Reay poet, Robert S. Stephen. The full work is published in Appendix 1 with the kind permission of the Stephen family.

2. From the Bee Gees song, 'First of May', recorded in November 1968 and released in March 1969. It was the penultimate track from *Odessa*, a double LP originally planned as a concept album about the loss of a fictional ship in 1899.

3. The photograph of Pilkington, reproduced with kind permission of the photographer, Evan Sutherland, Reay Golf Club.

4.   The originator of this verse is unknown. It is included in the unpublished notebooks of local archivist, Robert Stephen, and reproduced with the kind permission of the Stephen family.

5.   The lyrics from 'Come Dancing', written by Ray Davies and performed by the Kinks. It was first released as a single in November 1982.

6.   Chapter 5 of *The Muirfield Green: Muirfield and the Honourable Company* by George Pottinger.

7.   The British and International Golf Greenkeepers Association Limited, established to promote best practice in sports turf management.

Chapter

3

Further East

The captain, barely breathing,
Kneeling at the wheel.
Above him and beneath him,
Fifty thousand tons of steel.
Bob Dylan[1]

T he story of Reay Golf Club is a story of unsung
heroes—people who invested a disproportionate amount
of their time and energy, such that a vision might be
realised. Most golf clubs—indeed, most sporting endeavours—
depend on them. There are many in all walks of life; more than we
realise. Some of them will be buried in the graveyard immediately
on your left as you head further east from the entrance to the golf
course. There are many such small graveyards scattered across the

North Lands, each with their own stories to tell: Elizabeth at Balnakeil, Nik at Melness and the remarkable story of an ordinary life, a few miles back, George at Skerray. A monument to a memory, he is not there—a nowhere man.

Among the Skerray headstones is a touching tribute to another George Mackay, erected by his friends in London. Enough is known about young George to imagine his last days …

It was early morning, 12 April 1912. The house was slowly coming to life, and George was wide awake. In fitful excitement, he had hardly slept. Some last tearful farewells to the early morning maids, a final check that his tickets were secure in his pocket and quietly he slipped the safe moorings of 11 Queens Gate, Kensington, and his life as a footman. Emerging from the colonnaded porch, he touched the iron railings one last time, turned left, and then right onto Prince Consort Road, heading for Waterloo and the 07:45 train to Southampton. He was dressed in his Sunday-best suit and wearing a Sunday smile. He did not look back. The city was already bustling with the clatter of hooves and the too familiar smell of horse manure, soon to be replaced by the salt sea air he had known as a boy.

The young George had only just turned twenty, but already he had travelled far from his humble beginnings on a croft near Tongue, in Sutherland. One of twelve children to William and Christina Mackay, he was determined to better himself. Too often he had heard tales of regret, of lives half-lived in the bitter north. George, the Heilam ferryman, spoke of nothing else but his plans as a young man to travel to Canada and how he was persuaded to stay by the Duke of Sutherland. *This* George would not make the same mistake.

The third-class boat train from Waterloo pulled into Southampton Docks at 09:30, stopping at Berth 43/44. Clutching a small brown suitcase and ticket 42795, George alighted into the dockside sheds, crossed the road, controlled by a man with a red flag, and momentarily stood, awestruck by the sheer overwhelming size of the ship. It was beyond anything he could have imagined. Nothing like this was ever seen in the Kyle.

As a third-class passenger, George had a simple berth, shared with six other passengers. Keen to escape the claustrophobia of steerage and the company of strangers, many of whom could not speak English, he quickly found his way to the open decks. He was there when the ship cast off and was towed into the River Test by tugboats, there for the near collision with USMS *New York*, there when Cherbourg appeared on the French coast and there when the ship set sail for Cobh in the dim light of an April evening. All the while he grasped ticket 42795. It had cost £7 11*s*, all his savings, but he was bound for Rochester and a new life in Detroit. Of one thing he was certain: he was never going home.

Erected

IN LOVING MEMORY OF

GEORGE WILLIAM MACKAY

CLAICKBEA

SON OF

WILLIAM AND CHRISTINA MACKAY

WHO WAS LOST IN THE TITANIC

DISASTER, 15TH APRIL 1912

AGED 20 YEARS

"BLESSED ARE THE PURE IN HEART

FOR THEY SHALL SEE GOD," MATT V, VIII

A few hundred yards along from the golf course entrance, heading east and on the right, there is the much older Reay graveyard. On the opposite side is Cavendish Cottage, the last home of Robert Stephen, secretary of the old golf club until its demise in 1940. A polymath, Robert was also the part-time greenkeeper, acted as local archivist, was a keen photographer and an accomplished poet. One of his best works, 'Sunset Soliloquy', relates to Sandside Head, the headland to the western side of Sandside Bay, which is visible from nearly all the holes on Reay golf course. Local heroes abound:

> *I hear the voice of the restless sea,*
> *I must answer its age-old call;*
> *And I must climb old Sandside Head*
> *'Ere the gloaming shadows fall.* [2]

Further east from Cavendish Cottage, passing the gates of Dounreay prompts odd trains of thought. If I had lived my life backwards, I would now be living in the mid-1880s. The production motorcycle was in its infancy; George Eastman was on the cusp of producing the first Kodak camera; Karl Benz would launch the first petrol engine automobile; and Open golf was still in its infancy. A few more years and I would be in the reign of Tom Morris Senior and Tom Morris Junior. The passions that consume me had barely been invented. Instead, I was born in an electromechanical era, when we had harnessed the power to destroy worlds without the complexity of microcontroller circuits to oversee their operation. I marvel that we have survived.

There is a secret bunker at Hack Green, near Nantwich. You cannot miss it; there are signposts everywhere. It is an exhibition which only serves to demonstrate how close we came to Armageddon. I recognised much of the Post Office-sourced telecommunications equipment that was the best that money could buy. I can only testify to its supreme unreliability. Alarmingly and unsurprisingly, the Russians were no better.

I do not remember Monday, 26 September 1983, as being anything other than a very ordinary day. I probably listened to Mike Read on Radio 1 while driving into work; he probably played Culture Club's chart-topping Karma Chameleon[3] at some stage during his two-hour show—*I'm a man without conviction, I'm a man who doesn't know*. Fortunately, for the sake of mankind, there are those who *have* conviction and those who *do* know. Stanislav Petrov was one such man.

Born in Vladivostok, in 1939, Petrov was the son of a Second World War fighter pilot. He studied at the Kiev Military Aviation Engineering Academy, and after graduating in 1972, he eventually worked for the Soviet Air Defence Forces organisation responsible for developing and operating the Ballistic Missile Early Warning

System. On that ordinary Monday morning, sat in the Serpukhov-15 bunker outside Moscow, just three weeks after Korean Air Lines Flight 007 had been shot down by a Soviet Su-15 Interceptor, Petrov's radar screen displayed five intercontinental ballistic missiles heading from the US towards the Soviet Union. Fortunately for mankind, he had his doubts. He was not convinced by the reliability of the early warning system, and it seemed unlikely that the US would launch an all-out attack with just five missiles. "I couldn't move. I felt like I was sitting on a hot frying pan." He sat tight on his very hot seat until it became clear that it was a false alarm. It was eventually determined that the erroneous display had been created by a rare alignment of sunlight on high-altitude clouds above North Dakota.

The world was saved by a shift pattern. Unlike Petrov, all his colleagues were professional soldiers with a purely military background. Had they been on shift instead of Petrov, they would have followed procedure and reported the missile strike. His superiors would have launched an assault against the US, who would have responded in kind. Goodbye, cruel world.

Petrov was praised for his decision but also received a reprimand *for insufficiently documenting his actions*. He received awards and commendations from foreign organisations but nothing from his home country. His statue should be everywhere.

As I continue beyond the entrance to Dounreay, I wonder just how much our control systems have improved since 1983. I wonder what set of freak circumstances, civilian or military, might lead to another rare alignment of sunlight on high-altitude clouds.

Beyond Dounreay the A836 traverses an unremarkable landscape, briefly twisting as it crosses the Forss Water before descending into Thurso, with Dunnet Head on the horizon to the north-east. Thurso is the northernmost town on the British mainland and, as a terminus for the Sutherland and Caithness Railway—opened in 1874—is as far north as you can go by rail. For such an out-of-the-way place it is surprisingly lively, assisted by the proximity of Dounreay, the fishing industry and the ferries at nearby Scrabster; it is a gateway to the northern isles. Approaching the town centre from the west, a sharp right turn up the arrow-straight Princes Street eventually leads to the simple, purposeful station building, in essence an engine shed which sits parallel to the River Thurso. From here it is almost tempting to take to the rails for Wick.

The furthest north of the Far North Line, the single-track spur runs seven miles from Thurso down to Georgemas Junction, roughly parallel to the A9 and River Thurso. At the junction it joins the main line—161 miles of single track connecting Wick in the east with Inverness in the south. At the time of writing, there are just four trains each way per day connecting Wick and Inverness. In modern times the line does well to survive, but during both wars it provided an essential service for the military.

Instigated in 1917 by Sir John Jellicoe, commander of the Grand Fleet, the *Jellicoe Express* linked the south of England and Thurso. Heading north, it enabled the transfer of Royal Navy personnel to the British Fleet in Scapa Flow, while heading south it transported Scottish army recruits heading to the English ports and then mainland Europe. The 'express' squeezed up to 600 soldiers and seaman onto each train; it was neither a comfortable nor popular journey. It is estimated that over 500,000 military personnel were

42

transferred over these isolated tracks in the far north; a stark contrast to the near-empty carriages that ply these same rails in modern times.

For a significant part of the twentieth century, long-distance travel across the UK meant the train. During the war years, civilians were actively discouraged from travelling by rail.

In the summer of 1941 a year had passed since the Dunkirk evacuation, and the immediate scare of invasion had subdued. In the east the Germans were encircling Leningrad for the beginnings of a siege that would last 872 days and cost in excess of 632,000 lives. Nothing was certain; none of the outcomes we now take for granted were known. Anything could happen.

That same summer, my father was completing his final year at university. Evacuated to Cambridge from Queen Mary College, London, the previous year—in late 1940 or early 1941—he had applied for a position at ICI (Imperial Chemical Industries) Manchester and made the trip north for an interview. The wartime rail trip resulted in an offer of employment subject to him obtaining a first- or second-class honours degree. Dad's commencing salary as an industrial chemist would be £275 per annum with a £24 war supplement, working for either the Explosives Group (Billingham or Ardeer) or Dyestuffs Group (Blackley or Trafford Park). The offer letter also included this standard caveat:

In view of the company's promise to make every possible effort to reinstate those of its employees on 3 September 1939 who serve with the Colours, the question of retention in the company's service after the war of any employees engaged since that date must be subject to the prior claim of those individuals.

Nothing was certain.

In the early summer of 1941 he would pack up his few belongings and return to his parents' home in Andover to await the exam results. A short bike ride across town to his girlfriend's house would have helped fill the waiting hours—a welcome simplicity after the years of wartime travel to and from Cambridge.

I am surprised by what happened next, just a few days after his girlfriend's eighteenth birthday. Dad was extremely capable, studious and meticulous. Popular, good at games and fiercely loyal, he was nevertheless a reserved character who never drank and would have found himself in the kitchen at parties. There would have been no distractions. The disappointment and foreboding when the news came would have been intense—he had only achieved a B.Sc. pass degree. It was an event resurrected down the years in heated parental debates.

A telegram was sent to ICI Blackley. Agonising days later a letter postmarked Blackley, Manchester, 23 August 1941, landed on the doormat at Rooksbury Road, Andover:

Dear Mr Down,

We are writing to thank you for your telegram and confirmatory letter dated 20 August advising us that you only obtained a pass degree in your recent B.Sc. examination.

In normal circumstances this would disqualify you for a position with us, but we have referred to the notes which we made during the interview and have decided to make an exception in your case. In the attached formal letter, we are making you a conditional offer of a post at our Trafford Park Works, and if all is well, we will expect you to start with us on Monday, 1 September.

We feel sure that your work will justify the confidence we are placing in you ...

The formal letter contained some further conditions: the reinstatement priority for staff who served with the Colours, a medical examination and the following:

It is understood that our offer and your acceptance of employment are subject to your final allocation to the company by the Allocation Committee of the Military Recruiting Department of the Ministry of Labour.

In the dark days of 1941, this vaguely Orwellian government department was tasked with balancing the manpower needs of the Register of Protected Establishments with those of the armed forces; that summer both were suffering significant shortages. On 23 August 1941 final allocation to ICI was by no means certain.

TRAFFORD PARK WORKS COUNCIL 1947/1948.
Back row - K.Down;N.Mitchell;E.Royle;A.Oxley;A.Mosley;J.Rigby;G.Millar;
J.Balfour (Secretary).
Front row - J.Kidd;F.Burgess;Mrs M.A.Worthington;C.Wenyon;(Chairman).
Mrs E.Jordan;J.Dowd;G.Hickson.

Dad started with Dyestuffs Group at Trafford Park on 1 September 1941, staying with the company until his retirement, forty years later. He married his Andover girlfriend in 1943, and nine months later my sister arrived. The war ended, and eventually, perhaps with some reluctance on my mother's part, I made my appearance. In August 1941 none of this was known. Anything could happen.

Georgemas Junction, like many of the stops on the Sutherland and Caithness Railway, is conveniently placed for almost nothing. Its primary *raison d'etre* is to provide a link between the mainline running to Wick and the Thurso branch line. Trains arriving from Inverness will reverse up to Thurso from Georgemas before heading back down the line and terminating at Wick.

In recent years a more significant role has been established for Georgemas Junction, as evidenced by the 110-tonne gantry crane which has replaced the former up-platform. The crane enables the road-rail transfer of radioactive material from Dounreay to Sellafield for reprocessing.

Arriving at Wick, the rail traveller is deposited south of the river, a few hundred yards from the town centre but more than 3 miles from the golf course at Reiss, north of the town and the airport. By road from Thurso, follow the A9 to north of Georgemas, where it crosses the B874, signposted *Gillock*. Follow the B874 for approximately 14 miles, and then turn left onto the A99, east of the airport, signposted *John O'Groats, 16 miles*. Head north-east for 1.5 miles, and turn right following the signage marked *Golf Course, Reiss Sands and Reiss Lodge*. Looping around a farm, the course is less than a mile from the A99 and but a few yards from the sea—a perfect location.

Notes

1. Bob Dylan's 'Tempest', from the 2012 album of the same name. The song tells a story of the Titanic sinking and borrows heavily from the Carter Family's recording of *The Titanic*.

2. A further extract from 'Sunset Soliloquy' by local Reay poet, Robert S. Stephen. The full work is published in Appendix 1 with the kind permission of the Stephen family.

3. 'Karma Chameleon' was released in September 1983 in the UK; it spent six weeks at number one. Boy George claims it is a song about the fear of alienation—something not immediately obvious from the lyrics, nor its jaunty production.

Reiss Links

I dream of wires, the old days
New ways, new ways
I dream of wires
Robert Palmer[1]

Chapter 4

O
n a good day, with the sun on my back, I will stand at the
tee of a par 3, usually the twelfth at Allendale, and
imagine my delight as the ball gently rolls into the hole
for an ace. Such mental distractions are almost certain to guarantee
a double bogey. In 1967, at the Dunlop Masters, Tony Jacklin
famously aced the par 3 sixteenth at Royal St George's. At the end
of the round, he was approached by a senior member swaying to
and fro in the wind as his braces took the strain:

"You're Jacklin, aren't you?"
"Yes, sir."

"Did a hole in one at the sixteenth I hear."

"Yes, sir."

"Well done. What club did you use?"

"Six-iron, sir."

"Six-iron? Wrong club."[2]

Similar conversations are the preserve of senior members at all golf clubs. An ageing stalwart of the Allendale membership maintains that a par 3 birdie takes more skill than an ace, the latter being entirely attributable to luck. Analysing this philosophy more closely, it must surely depend on the proximity of the ball to the cup—anything within 3 feet again being pure luck, and anything outside being solid golf demanding of a sure and steady putt. Invariably, I will miss the green entirely, recover the situation, sometimes, with a well-struck lob and then a two-putt for a net par; four shots, each demanding different levels of skill and determination, without the merest hint of good fortune. Our senior member must surely have a point—aces take no skill at all, and on this basis one must be heading my way very soon.

As I stand on the first tee at Wick, I note that there will be five opportunities to bag my first hole-in-one. As ever, I set off in a positive frame of mind. As ever, I wonder how long this optimism can last. In truth, holes-in-one are not high on my agenda; a good solid round is all I ask.

The Wick course follows a familiar links format: a north-heading outward eight, hugging the landward side of the course, an east-facing ninth par 3 at its furthest reaches and a return nine running south and parallel to the mutinous sand dunes that divide the course from Sinclair's Bay. For those members or visitors short on time or energy there is a formally assessed

9-hole, par 35 course which goes north as far as hole five and returns to the clubhouse from holes fifteen through eighteen.

To play this nine is to tread similar ground to the original 9-hole course first established in 1870.

Succinctly named *Angle, Cross, Long, End, Bent, Cable, Plain, Tower* and *Home*, the poetry was reserved for the bunkers, not least the monstrous *Hades* which had to be negotiated from the second tee.

The July 1904 edition of *Golf Illustrated* describes it as *a yawning sand bunker which necessitates a carry of about 140 yards. It is so close to the tee that there is no escape for a topped shot; in it must go, and the player who forgets that extrication is the first duty in a bunker and attempts the heroic is likely to regret his rashness. The carry is, of course, not too much for fair swiping, and once over, all that should remain is a careful approach.*[3]

Sadly, *Hades* is no more; at least not in this world. Also gone is a style of golf reportage that includes a *fair swiping* within its lexicon, even though it seems a more accurate description of my golf swing than any other I have heard. The image[4] below shows an early golfer facing up to the challenge of *Hades*, adopting a stance synonymous with *all forward and trust in the Lord*—divine intervention being required to ensure the necessary carry.

Other hazards included the *Duffers* bunker, the *Hedgehog* mound, a deep ditch named *Styx* and the ominously labelled sand bunker, *Purgatory*. Inevitably, much has changed between the original 9-hole course and the present-day layout, but there is one constant throughout. Examine the image of *Hades*, and in the distance is the small building and associated telegraph pole indicating the point where an underwater cable comes ashore. Originally the location of the 9-hole sixth green, named *Cable*, it is now the sixteenth green and named *Cable House*.

In this overly connected world, we take person-to-person communication for granted. There are now such myriad ways to say hello and broadcast inconsequential stuff to the world, that it is easy to forget how limited our options once were. Most of the girlfriends from my teenage years only had access to a public telephone. Dates were made long in advance, and arrangements demanded memory and commitment, depending on your inclination. It was easy to forget and easy to be forgotten.

Christmas 1972, and I bought her Joni Mitchell's *Blue*, and she bought me Santana's *Caravanserai*. Seven days previously I had offered a cigarette, and we took it from there. What do the young do now? Buy an iTunes voucher and offer an organic carrot? Where is the history? Where is love's private audit trail?

I worked shifts at the University of Manchester Regional Computing Centre on Oxford Road. The route to work was by train from Altrincham and then a short walk from Station Approach to the computer centre, passing an array of guitar shops, the discreet family-planning outlet under the railway arch and the Regal Cinema, rebranded as Studio 1 to 5, which that summer was prophetically screening Peter Bogdanovich's *The Last Picture Show*. All of this is gone.

Thanks to the endless trivia available on the Internet, I know this to be true. On Tuesday, 19 June 1973, I was working the late shift, and when *The Old Grey Whistle Test* was broadcast that evening, I was having a fag break in the rest lounge. I do not know what struck me first, the music or the video—a black and white montage of formation skiers in descent, which as one online reference claims is Nazi propaganda. I was hooked and the next day went in search of the LP. Released on 25 May by Virgin; the record was Mike Oldfield's *Tubular Bells*. Fags, LPs and public telephone boxes were the passport to many things. A life without them would have been unthinkable.

From the personal effects of my courting parents, it seems they wrote letters but rarely exchanged postcards, their intimate content being too accessible to prying eyes. Communication across a war-torn country—my father in Cambridge and my mother in Andover—must have been less than reliable, so in emergency they would resort to telegram, a terse form of communication constrained by per-word charging.

When the Orkney & Shetland Islands Telegraph Company installed a 260-mile cable from Wick to the Shetland Islands via Orkney, their charges varied between two and three shillings for twenty words, later rising to six shillings. Words did not come cheap. Now, at any moment in time, billions of words encircle the Earth at no cost to the originator. Amid all this noise and chatter there will be wisdom and truth. The challenge in the twenty-first century is to find it.

It would be a modern conceit to imagine that global electronic communication is a recent invention. As early as 1891, *Leslie's Monthly*, an illustrated magazine published in New York, featured the story of Cyrus Field, the New York businessman whose efforts were largely responsible for the installation of the first Atlantic telegraph cables. It describes two aspects of telegraphy in Britain:[5]

> *The British government has 103 cables around its shores of a total length of 1,489 miles. If we include India and the colonies, the British Empire owns altogether 216 cables of a total length of 3,811 miles.*

> *The longest government cable in British waters is that from Sinclair Bay, Wick, to Sandwick Bay, Shetland, of the length of 122 miles and laid in 1885; the shortest being four cables across the Gloucester and Sharpness Canal, at the latter place, and each less than 300 feet in length.*

It is this, *the longest government cable*, that used to make landfall at the sixth green, now the sixteenth, and resulted in the construction of the cable house, the transition point between the undersea cable and the landline telegraph wires which carried the signal to the cable office at Wick.

The high dunes, the stone hut, the telegraph post adjacent to the seventeenth tee, the broad sweep of Sinclair's Bay and the distant castle silhouettes are the iconic ingredients of Wick golf course that remain in the memory long after the final putt at the eighteenth, the saddest stroke of the day.

The modern course has its roots in the 1907 extension to eighteen holes, designed by John Sutherland, secretary of the Royal Dornoch Golf Club for fifty-eight years. He was commissioned to examine the course with a view to extension in 1906. John went over the ground in mid-November and duly wrote to the club with recommendations on 24 November. A copy of the detailed letter is still in the possession of the club.

In five A4 pages of a clear and methodical hand, John not only describes his recommendations for the extension but details precisely how the rabbit scrapings can be repaired, the fairways made playable and the greens constructed. There is no mention of earth moving and no tinkering with the natural landscape—the course would be played as God intended.

In his own words: *As to the course, I have tried to get it to run on the most approved lines, out by the left and in by the left, without a crossing. There is a crossing, however, at the second hole, but it is not a dangerous one, and as long as there is no danger, a good hole should not be discarded because of a crossing.*

On 2 March 1907, the Extension Committee convened on the course, fixed the tee and green positions, measured each hole and gave instructions to the greenkeeper to have them made. The committee had followed John's recommendations, with only minor deviations. On that early Spring day of 1907, the seeds of a new course were sown on Reiss links. At 5,078 yards it is just a few hundred yards short of the current red tees.

With only minor changes over the years, the John Sutherland-inspired layout would remain at the heart of the Wick course layout until club captain, John Hunter, instigated some significant course amendments in 2002, endorsed by Ronan Rafferty. These most recent changes finally eliminated the drive over the second green from the seventeenth tee, an oddity which resulted in some frustration when the course was busy. Much more remarkable is the course's survival beyond 1945.

From Keiss Castle to Noss Head, Sinclair's Bay sweeps around this north-east coast in a seven-mile arc. At the outbreak of the Second World War, the bay was regarded as a strategic landing option for a German invasion from the north. The wide-open bay would provide perfect territory for a massed landing, while just a few miles south, Wick airfield would provide an ideal northern base for the Luftwaffe.

The golf course closed in the winter of 1940, and in the early months of 1941 the Royal Engineers started to lay 2,000 beach mines in a continuous belt, 3.5 miles long by 50 yards wide, from Keiss to Ackergill. The minefield was believed to be the largest in the UK. In addition to the minefield, barriers were constructed along the dunes and anti-tank mines and a flame barrage were put in place at the Burn of Wester, the northernmost reach of the golf course. The flame barrage consisted of large tanks, situated behind the dunes, which held a mixture of oil and petrol. In the event of an invasion, a network of pipes would flood the beach with this highly flammable mixture and the sands would ignite. It would have been a spectacular show, and there must have been sappers just itching to try it out. However, as history tells us, these defences were never tested, and at the end of the conflict what remained was a huge clean-up exercise.

The removal of mines, some buried up to 15 feet by shifting sands, would take two years. Various methods were employed, but a report in *The Scotsman*, dated 20 September 1946, suggests a modicum of frustration with the slow methods used for much of the clearance activity. A system of water-jetting for removal of sand from the top of the mine was deemed unnecessary when it was discovered that the mines could be detonated by placing small charges on top.

> *It was therefore decided to detonate the whole minefield by this method simultaneously—and the neighbourhood looked forward apprehensively to a small-scale Bikini.[6] The sand muffled the effects of the explosion which succeeded, however, in detonating almost all the mines in the field.*

> *Unfortunately, during later clearances, blast carried by one detonation was sufficient to damage the clubhouse roof at Reiss golf course. The work has been carried on recently by German prisoners of war,[7] for whose employment on this work special permission was given by the Foreign Office on condition that adequate training was first given and due precautions were observed.*

According to the *Sunday Post* published on 26 May 1946, this was not the first such occurrence:

> *Explosion of mines recovered by sappers from a wartime minefield in the sand dunes adjoining the course at Reiss ...*

*raised the clubhouse roof several inches from the walls. The
club is taking immediate steps to secure the roof in case the
next explosion whisks it away altogether.*

However, repairs to the clubhouse roof were the least of the
problems for the golf club. All the activity during the war,
including troop training exercises, and the post-war mine
clearance had done enormous damage to the links. A schedule of
works drawn up by the club included repair to infrastructure items,
such as fences, gates and sheds, and much of the playing surface,
not surprisingly, greens and bunkers. In addition to materials and
supervision costs, the schedule specified 2,546 man hours to
undertake the work at roughly two shillings per hour—the
equivalent of nearly £20,000 at current minimum wage rates.
When submitted to the MOD for compensation, they rejected the
manpower charge but offered to provide labour by use of prisoners
of war based at nearby Camp 165 Watten, the same resource that
had recently been used for mine removal.

There would have been a certain moral justice at work if those
who had sown the seeds of destruction had laboured to deal with
the consequences. Unsurprisingly, the worst of them would be
the least trusted and confined to the high-security parts of the
camp. It was the foot soldiers, the bystanders caught up in
history, who worked to repair the greens and fairways at Reiss.
Oddly, a course destroyed by the British Army was resurrected
by the German.

Watten opened in August 1943 as a military training camp and
continued in that role until May 1945 when the first German
prisoners of war arrived. Transported by train and truck to the far
north, many had been captured in Normandy as the Allies

advanced through France. *The prisoners destined for Watten were both the innocents caught up by Hitler's propaganda machine and the notorious for their fastidious belief in the Third Reich's place in the world and its domination of that world. When they were dropped off at the railway platform by the loch and marched up to the main camp, their lives were about to change.*[8]

The compound was divided into two areas: A and B. Category A prisoners were assessed as low threat and eventually allowed off-camp to perform unpaid work for local farmers. This is the same group of prisoners that would assist with mine clearance at Reiss links and undertake repairs to the golf course. However, Category B prisoners were an altogether different kettle of fish; housed in top-secret Area B, overseen by armed guards and watch towers, they were known as the 'black' prisoners. They were hard line, dangerous and subjected to de-Nazification programmes—an optimistic endeavour, the results of which must have been near impossible to accurately assess.

It would be reassuring to believe that the nasty brigade[4] finally got their comeuppance, but the stories of the more notorious inmates suggest otherwise. Paul Werner Hoppe, the commandant of Stutthof concentration camp, escaped, worked as a landscape gardener in Saxony until 1953, was rearrested and served just nine years' imprisonment. Dr Paul Schroder, responsible for the Nazi's V2 flying bomb project which wreaked havoc over London, gained privileges and special treatment by sharing his knowledge of advanced rocketry. He eventually worked for the US Air Force. Hitler's personal aide, and SS commander, Max Wunsche, returned to Germany in 1947 and was immediately released. He died in 1995. Nazi propagandist, Gunter d'Alquen, was sent to the US, where he became a key member of the CIA. U-boat captain, Otto Kretschmer, known as the 'Wolf of the Atlantic', was released in December 1947. He joined the newly formed Bundesmarine in 1955, eventually becoming chief of staff of the NATO command, Allied Forces Baltic Approaches.

Nobody gets justice. People only get good luck or bad luck. (Orson Welles)

The course is lit by a brilliant spring light, cotton wool clouds fill the sky and a modest breeze blows from south to north—a following wind for the front nine.

Press a tee into the soft Caithness turf at the first, and this now seems like sacred ground. The view north is serene, the vista so wide and empty, and yet just beneath the surface there are ghostly footprints. The early golfers, the sappers, the squaddies, the prisoners of war, all have trodden this ground. Straight down the middle it measures 6,123 yards off the whites and 5,777 yards off the yellows; as a casual visitor, yellow is the colour for all the references to distance.

Holes one and two, the par 4 *First* and the par 3 *Hunters Joy*, offer a gentle introduction at 277 yards and 148 yards respectively—avoid pulling the drives left and keep out of the bunkers, and early pars are possible. Heading further north, the third, *Quoys*, is the first of the par 5s, which crosses a burn, and with a slight dog-leg left reaches the green in 501 yards. With a following wind, the swing

feels easy, the world a wonderful place, and my ball flies unheard-of distances with the kind of consistency usually reserved for dreams. Would this all be so entertaining if that element of mystery and surprise were entirely removed from my game? Does the professional experience the same level of joy when things go well?

Bearing in mind that John Sutherland, when making his recommendations for the 18-hole extension, was writing in 1906 and using equipment, clubs and balls, with nothing like the capabilities of modern equipment, it is astonishing to realise that his course measurements were simply based on how far he could hit the ball—*All of the distances given are approximate, judged by my driving balls. As the ball played was a Goodrich Tournament, which I now find does not get the distance of the Kite or Colonel, the distances may be rather overstated.*

My distances would be entirely arbitrary, regardless of the ball used.

The tee box for the fourth, *Knowe*, a 193-yard par 3, is adjacent to the third green. The hole is protected by front bunkers left and right, while out-of-bounds all the way down the left encourages a shot to the right. In early spring the rough was thin and forgiving; later in the year I guess it would offer a more demanding hazard.

The joy of the long-hit ball continues through a series of par 4s, *Sleepers*, *Warren* and *Wester*, where the predominant hazard remains out-of-bounds to the left, the occasional burn crossing the fairway and the greenside bunkers. The journey north finishes with the eighth, a fine par 5, *River*. At 500 yards, favourable conditions should mean finding the green in regulation. Avoid the three-putt on the typically excellent green, and another par is there for the taking. At this, its most northerly point, the course turns seaward, where the River Wester flows from the Loch of Wester and makes for the briny. The aptly named *Tern*, a short 134-yard par 3 to a raised green, completes the front nine. On the higher ground, at the edge of the dunes, the view south takes in the return journey, and the view north speaks of the ancient and the modern.

Immediately north there are the remains of an Iron Age broch at Castle Linglas, and on the horizon beyond, the remains of the sixteenth-century Keiss Castle. However, in between and just north of the broch, Subsea 7 is in a similar business to the pioneers who laid the first telegraph cables to Orkney and beyond. This unique site stretches nearly 5 miles inland and manufactures pipes and pipeline bundles of up to 4.8 miles in length for the oil and gas extraction industry. Assembled in the inland fabrication shops, the bogie-mounted, welded pipes run down to the shore on four discreet railway tracks, with a near total capacity of 17 miles. A launch way enables them to be delivered to their destination using the Controlled Depth Tow Method, a towing operation where the pipe, string or bundle is made almost buoyant and towed at a controlled depth suspended between a lead and trail tug. This is large scale manufacturing at technology's leading edge, and it is happening on the remote shores of Sinclair's Bay.

Nathaniel John Holmes would gaze upon this technology with envious eyes. In the same year that Wick Golf Club was established, he became engineer to the Orkney & Shetland Islands Telegraph Company, laying cables from Wick to Shetland via the coastal station of Voe in Caithness, a precursor to the telegraph cable that emerges at the sixteenth. Undertaken with the Siemens Brothers, laying cables across the Pentland

Firth was such a dreadful experience, that he was prompted to design and patent instantaneously igniting signal flares and maritime air horns for saving lives at sea. Nathaniel then established his own company dedicated to their production, the grandly named Holmes' Marine Life Protection Association, an undertaking so successful, that it would eventually become part of the Albright & Wilson empire.[9]

It would seem that Nathaniel was a man with a keen eye for a good explosion. In 1863 he was responsible for establishing the Glasgow time gun. *The Greenock Advertiser* of 28 November in the same year relates that:

> *On Wednesday, at the Central Police Court, Glasgow, before Bailie Grant, Mr Nathaniel John Holmes, engineer to the Universal Private Telegraph Company, was charged with contravening the Glasgow Police Act 1862, in so far as on 16 November he wantonly discharged a cannon or other firearm from the roof of a building situated at St Vincent Place, the discharge of said cannon being to the annoyance or danger of passengers or persons carrying on business in the neighbourhood. The procurator fiscal urged the danger to the public from the startling of horses in a crowded thoroughfare and also the danger of fire from the ignited wadding being scattered about.*

You would think twice before letting the man loose near a flame barrage.

The aerial photograph is the view north, with the fifth and thirteenth greens in the foreground.[10]

As I turn and head south into the prevailing wind, the brilliant spring light has lost its shine, the skies are threatening and the wind is rising. These conditions taught me a fundamental truth about the flight of my ball from the tee: every drive shares the characteristics of that most affectionate of lapdogs, the Irish Setter. With a following wind, it will fly arrow straight to a far destination which may or may not be the one intended. By contrast, into the wind, and the olfactory senses are so overwhelmed by distractions, that it will dart left or right in a large sweeping arc, regardless how unpleasant the undergrowth. As became all too clear, my drives would emulate this trajectory exactly.

My front nine was more than respectable, and I wondered where this sudden gift had come from, only to find reality strike as I turned for home. The skies darkened, rain threatened, the wind buffeted my face and the solid front nine disappeared into a wayward damp return. For the average club golfer it is unwise to ever think you have finally cracked this game; if things are going well, there is probably an underlying reason, and the reason is sure to bite back sooner or later.

And so it was on this day. The slightly elevated tee at the tenth, the 380-yard *Bay View*, overlooks the Wester estuary and tempts a 'fair swiping'. With a natural tendency to fade, more commonly called slice, the rough to the right of this dog-leg left was my inevitable destination for this and many of the other holes on the back nine. That I contrived to play the same ball throughout says more about the thinness of the rough in a Caithness spring than any innate skill.

The 166-yard, par 3 eleventh, *Shochad*, is relatively straight-forward, whereas the stroke index 2, par 4 twelfth, *March*, seemed anything but. As the wind increased yet more, the glasses began to mist and the distance to the far clubhouse seemed never to diminish. It is perhaps the clearest indication of the madness afflicting the average golfer that we will continue regardless of the conditions and regardless of our limited abilities, which reduce in direct relation to the volume of water trickling down our necks. And it is not just the weather. Almost every golfer I know of a certain age is carrying a variety of injuries, none of which, no matter how serious, will keep us off the fairways. We pop pills, strap our joints with various items of torture and on we plough. Those busybodies at the Department of Work & Pensions will name and shame benefit claimants playing golf as evidence of fitness for work. Have they no idea of the agonies we are going through? This is not sport; this is religion—the seeking of sanctity through mortification of the flesh. By the end of the round I feel confident I will be elevated to sainthood.

Another par 4 of similar length, *Cup*, follows at the thirteenth, followed by the light relief of a par 3, *Plateau*. At stroke index 18, it is supposedly the easiest hole on the course, at 148 yards, but I confess I found hitting the greens on the front nine par 3s significantly easier. As the name suggests, getting the ball to stick on this green is a challenge.

From here on it is par 4s all the way to the clubhouse: *Desert*, followed by *Cable House*, followed by *Sinclair Bay*, followed by *Home*. In the shadow of the high dunes, the sixteenth leads you down to the iconic telegraph pole and stone building.

The seventeenth tee is mounted in a gap in the dunes just north of the telegraph pole, with the full sweep of Sinclair's Bay visible north and south. It is an arresting sight. My shape of shot into a prevailing wind demands a drive over the edge of the dunes, a ball that will disappear as it bends to hunt the short grass. Is there a better feeling in the world than seeing your ball plumb-centre of the fairway after a blind drive? It is like being reconnected with a wayward offspring.

In a lighter mood, I par the seventeenth and only miss repeating the trick when I three-putt the eighteenth. I have made it to *Home*, damp but not dispirited. Indeed, elevated by experiencing an exceptionally fine links course on perhaps not the finest of days.

The memory of this fine view[11] will linger, with or without a halo. *Au revoir*, Reiss Links. I will return.

Notes

1. The lyrics are from 'I Dream of Wires' by Robert Palmer, which appears on his solo album, *Clues* (1980), and on the compilation album, *Addictions Vol. 2* (1992).

2. This conversation was first published in *Golf Quarterly*, Issue 8, in the winter of 2012. It is an extract from the chapter on golf in Christopher Martin Jenkins' memoir, *CMJ: A Cricketing Life*.

3. An extract from the *Golf Illustrated* article, 15 July 1904, entitled 'Golf in the North of Scotland: Wick Golf Course'.

4. The image of golfers traversing *Hades* and Watten Camp prisoners is reproduced with the kind permission of The Wick Society Johnston Collection.

5. Information kindly researched and supplied by Bill Burns and Bill Glover of atlantic-cable.com.

6. The first of the Operation Crossroads atomic tests had taken place on the Bikini Atoll just a few months previously, on 1 July 1946.

7. The German prisoners of war were on day release from nearby Camp 165 Watten, which did not close until April 1948.

8. Chapter 1, 'Beginnings', *Camp 165 Watten* by Valerie Campbell.

9. Albright & Wilson was set up as a partnership between two Quakers, Arthur Albright and John Edward Wilson. The company was founded in 1856 as a United Kingdom manufacturer of potassium chlorate and white phosphorus for the match industry. It became a private limited company, Albright & Wilson Ltd, in 1892, and it remained a double-family-owned firm for nearly a hundred years, until 5 March 1948, when it became a public company.

10. The aerial drone image is reproduced with the kind permission of James McLeod.

11. The image is reproduced by kind permission of Andrew Simpson, a member of Wick Golf Club. It shows the view over the cable house towards the seventeenth fairway and clubhouse, with Ackergill Tower to the left.

Heading South

Chapter 5

*There is no real way to deal with
everything we lose.*
Joan Didion[1]

Finally, there is a sense of return. Leaving Reiss Links and picking up the A99, I am heading south. Beyond Wick town centre, the road hugs the coast for much of the route to Dornoch Firth, where it finally loses touch with the sea until reaching the shores of the Cromarty Firth.

By contrast, the railway south from Wick heads inland to avoid the major civil engineering challenge and associated cost of constructing a line over the Ord of Caithness. The consequence of this nineteenth-century decision is that the line travels remarkable distances to go to the very epicentre of the middle of nowhere. For the idle rail enthusiast with no desire other than to observe the empty majesty of the Flow Country, this is heaven. For the good people of Wick and Thurso, and a commercial enterprise dependent on attracting passenger traffic, it is not what the doctor ordered. For it to have survived post-Beeching is a minor miracle.

The Far North Line, from Wick to Inverness, has a well-documented poor-reliability record. Ageing rolling stock and a single track with insufficient passing loops means that disruption to one service snowballs across the rest. The occasional thump of shrubbery against windows also testifies to poor trackside maintenance.

However, the problem with the Far North Line runs much deeper than reliability. Travel by car from Wick to Inverness, and under normal circumstances it will take about two and half hours. Travel by rail, and it takes over four. It is all down to geography. The line takes the long route around three firths— Beauly, Cromarty and Dornie—such that the distance by rail is roughly twice that of a well-trained crow on a still day. All three firths are crossed by road bridges with no accommodation for rail. The diversion inland from Wick to Helmsdale just exacerbates the problem.

The coastal towns north of Helmsdale were not always so disconnected from the rail network. Examine the OS map and there is evidence of a dismantled railway running parallel to the A99 all the way down to Lybster.

The Wick and Lybster Light Railway conformed to the Light Railway Act of 1896, which did not demand specific legislation to construct. Reducing legal costs and enabling new railways to be built quickly, it was intended to encourage the building of new light railways in areas of low population. Using the powers of this

Act, the Wick and Lybster Light Railway finally opened on 1 July 1903, but with the new legislation came certain restrictions: the weight of the rolling stock could not exceed 12 tons on any one axle; the maximum speed was 25 mph, reducing to 10 mph on curves which had a radius of less than nine chains; and level crossings had to be approached at no more than 10 mph.

The decline of the fishing industry at Lybster and the construction of a road between Wick and Helmsdale in the 1930s signalled the end for the light railway, which closed on 1 April 1944. John Skene, who was the driver of the first train on the opening day of the railway in 1903, steamed up the engine for the last trip in 1944. Affectionately known as the 'Coffee Pot', the engine was given a rousing final send off. According to the *Aberdeen Press and Journal* of 3 April 1944:

> *Engine Beflagged—Many passengers made the journey on the train's last run. The engine was decked with flags for the occasion. All the way along the 13-mile journey past crofters' cottages and wayside stations people waved farewells and the engine's siren shrieked a response.*

Perhaps because of the harsh terrain and climate, perhaps because of its 'light' construction, little remains visible: the occasional embankment seen from the A99, the hint of a cutting through an empty field and maybe the odd stationmaster's house, indistinguishable from other Caithness architecture.

The wonderful exceptions are the station buildings at Thrumster and Lybster. Following the line's closure, Thrumster Station continued life as a post office, a caravan-site office and finally a garage store before being acquired by the Yarrows Heritage Trust[2] in 2005. It is now perfectly preserved internally and externally, defiantly sited just a few feet from the busy road heading north to Wick.

More remarkable still, the ticket office also survives at the line's terminus in its present guise: the clubhouse for the Lybster golf course. Located on an area of land called Black Park, the club pre-dates the arrival of the railway which split the course in two. For a time, the two co-existed, but within a year land was found south of the town and the club relocated to Reisgill Burn. A 1905 edition of *Golf Illustrated* describes a course that is *from 150 yards to 250 yards broad, and along the greater part of the course is bounded either side by steeply sloping banks, mostly covered with whin bushes ... The configuration of the ground and the winding*

*character of the banks combine to make the lower half of the
course more romantic and varied than golf courses usually are.*

It is not clear how long golf was played across this testing terrain,
but by December 1925 *The Scotsman* was reporting that Lybster
Golf Club was seeking to re-establish the course at Black Park, as
*there had been for some time a strong desire to form a golf club for
the use of the inhabitants and of summer visitors, and that, with
that object, a sum of over £300, sufficient to meet the expenditure
necessary to lay out a golf course, had been collected.*

So once again golf would be played close to the steaming Coffee
Pot, only this time it would be the railway that would eventually
vacate the plot. Over time the course was reconfigured, such that
the original clubhouse at the first green transferred to the old ticket
office and the future of the building was guaranteed. Sadly, the
platform is no more, but the stationmaster's house remains, and as
you play the top end of the course, you are traversing a cutting for
the old line.

The A99 becomes the A9 at Latheron, and I keep heading south. None of this is new to me. Long-distance travel by car for holidays across the UK were the happiest times of my childhood. My mother's unpredictability was tempered by the reassuring, all-day presence of my dad and, in the early years, my Aunt Bet, Uncle Ed and their son Brian. The first car I remember was a black Ford Consul Mk1, bought by my parents in June 1953. Bench seats, a column change, three forward gears, no heater, manual choke, a hard metal facia and a predisposition not to start in winter, it was the height of modernity. Its 1508cc inline, 4-cylinder engine would plod its way from 0–60 mph in a glacial 27.7 seconds, and yet only returned 25 miles to the gallon. It was neither nifty nor thrifty.

Following are some moments from the rear bench seat of the black Ford. Most memorable was my mother's overtaking manoeuvre in fog on the old A40 between Banbury and Oxford, which my dad had advised against. We avoided a head-on by the narrowest of narrow margins. My mother, parking the car in the middle of the A34, south of Newbury, announced she was leaving. Dad being Dad, he went to fetch her, while I was all for leaving her behind. In the heat of another argument, my mother, announcing she had had enough of this life, steered the car towards a ditch on the Chester Road, south of Altrincham. My dad, a man with sportsman's reactions, simultaneously grabbed the wheel and handbrake to avert disaster. The roads were quieter in those days, but I was, unsurprisingly, a boy of a nervous disposition in the company of my mother.

We were heading for North Wales in 1957 when my father captured this odd moment in time:

In a scene reminiscent of the Munsters, to the left Uncle Ed is stood to attention in his flat cap, as though about to preach a sermon, oblivious to the chaos around him. Unique in my experience, my sister has adopted my patent Quasimodo pose, while the bemused Brian is backing off in fear of this strange girl's antics. Aunt Bet is hiding in the shadows of her monstrous Jaguar SS, too sozzled[3] to emerge. Mother, washerwoman with arms folded (her description not mine), is in earnest conversation with Pop, who if I remember correctly, was stone deaf. I am putting on a performance while Dad is hiding behind the Kodak Brownie Cresta.

Time and fate were waiting in the wings. The older generation is gone. My sister would serve food and wine at icy altitudes and marry her jet pilot, I would spend a lifetime in a digital cloud and

Brian would become a leading AIDS doctor, treating stars whose bright lights would be extinguished too early: Denholm Elliott, Freddie Mercury and Kenny Everett. In 1957 much of the vocabulary to describe how we ended up making our living had yet to enter the common lexicon.

From Latheron, the A9 follows the coast south-west through Dunbeath to Helmsdale, where it meets up with the Far North Line again after its inland meanderings. Road and rail keep close company for the next 20 miles, passing close to Brora and Golspie golf courses, the proximity of rail and fairway making both ideal for enthusiasts of Scottish golf by train.[4]

As the A9 skirts the northern end of Loch Fleet, the railway passes beneath and heads inland again to Lairg, circumnavigating Beinn Domhnaill via Invershin and Ardgay, all to avoid the expense of bridging Dornoch Firth. The road bridge was completed in 1991 and reduced the route north by some 26 miles, but in so doing took northern travellers away from the traditional crossing at Bonar Bridge. As we increasingly rely on satnavs and less so on maps, it is all too easy to be unaware of the interesting diversion, and we are less likely to take the road less travelled. More and more we may know where we're going but have no idea where we've been. To miss Bonar Bridge, Ardgay would be a mistake. Two miles north of the new bridge, the old road parts company with the A9 near Clashmore, becomes the A949 and heads inland, signposted *Bonar Bridge, 10 miles*.

Until 1957 there was also an option to cross the Firth on the Meikle Ferry, a three-quarter mile, watery journey to the Ness of Portnaculter. A single-track road, about a mile south of the A949 turning, leads down to the old slipway, where an information board tells the tragic story of the 1809 disaster when the overcrowded ferry capsized in rough seas, drowning ninety-nine passengers returning from a day out at Tain market. Only locals, lost souls or nosey individuals pass this way now, but there are rewards for the inquisitive with a golfing bent.

To the north of the approach road, and for a short stretch to the south, there is evidence of a very grand golf course. It is the Carnegie Links, built on land to the south of Skibo Castle. There are no signs, no outward display of its existence, the implication being if you don't know it is there, you don't need to. *There are no tee times at Skibo, so members are free to play as and when the mood takes them.*[5] The same applies at Allendale.

Andrew Carnegie, the immensely rich steel magnate and philanthropist, returned to his country of birth in the late nineteenth century, acquired Skibo Castle and invested millions of dollars in its renovation. Undertaken to provide a home in Scotland and a legacy for his daughter, it remained in the family until 1982. The magnificent castle and grounds now form the basis of the Carnegie Club, which includes a very fine 18-hole links course.

Carnegie was a keen fisherman and golfer. These two passions were combined within the bounds of the Skibo estate. Firstly, he dammed the River Evelix to create a trout and salmon loch of over half a mile in length, and then, to the south of the new waters, he laid out a 9-hole golf course. Thus, in a single day he could conveniently net grilse, sea trout and brown trout and post a respectable golf score. Writing in 1907, John Sutherland,[6] who was responsible for laying out the nine holes, considered it too short and too easy but prophetically observed it had *ample room for extension*. Following Carnegie's death in 1919, the course was abandoned. According to the Carnegie Club archivist,[7] *we know very little about the original 9-hole course. While the course was well used by Carnegie during his time at Skibo, it fell into disuse over the course of the twentieth century and was gone by the time the estate was sold by the Carnegie family in 1982—the Savills sales brochure from this time makes no mention of a golf course. My understanding is that the clubhouse burned down in the mid-1930s.*

The course remained overgrown until resurrected in 1990 by a new owner, Peter de Savary. Another change of ownership in 2003 resulted in the commissioning of further radical enhancements, and the course as it is presented today is laid out on the links land between the artificial Loch Evelix and the Kyle of Sutherland. Members of the Carnegie Club still access the course by the carriage road which sits on top of the embankment separating the waters of the loch from the sea.

Returning to the A949, the entrance to Skibo Castle, one mile from the A9 junction, is as discreet as the golf course. Continuing towards Bonar Bridge, the largely traffic-free road is eerily quiet, lined with trees on the northward side and open views across Dornoch Firth on the southward side. This lonely road is reason enough to be diverted. Arriving in the town, a row of tidy houses leads to the modern bridge, the third of its kind. Where once drovers forded cattle across the Kyle, Thomas Telford's cast-iron bridge spanned the water between 1812 and 1892, when it was swept away by flood water. By 1973 its triple-arched replacement was deemed too weak and was replaced by the modern structure. Directly opposite the bridge, Migdale Road leads to the high ground above the town, and half a mile up on the right is the entrance to Bonar Bridge, Ardgay Golf Club, a fine course with some illustrious connections. *Golf in the Wild* returns to its roots: a testing 9-hole tract in an out-of-the-way place.

Notes

1.   A quote from Joan Didion's 2003 memoir, *Where I was From*, first published in Great Britain by Flamingo and described by Blake Morrison as *an elegy for lost innocence.*

2.   Yarrows Heritage Trust was formed to preserve and enhance access to all aspects of Yarrow's historical, cultural and natural heritage. The trust takes its name from an area of upland that extends from Thrumster to Clyth in the south.

3.   Poetic licence—I do not remember any of them ever drinking more than a sherry at Christmas. Money was too tight to mention, and alcohol was never one of life's essentials.

4.   This not-so-rare breed of enthusiast inspired David Crossley to establish the excellent website: www.scottishgolfbytrain.co.uk.

5.   A quote from The Carnegie Club website. Play it as it lies—over 6,833 yards of golfing genius.

6.   Based on articles published by John Sutherland and reproduced in *Golf Causerie,* 25 October 1907, Andrew Carnegie as a sportsman. This is the same John Sutherland who had much to do with the 1907 extension of the Wick course to eighteen holes.

7.   A wealth of information was kindly supplied by Victoria Connor, the Carnegie Club archivist. Sadly, all trace of the original course has been lost; there is no detail of the layout, nor a scorecard, to give any indication of its length/structure.

Bonar Bridge

*Everybody must give something
back for something they get.*[1]
Bob Dylan

In conversations stretching over several summers in the late 1800s, Andrew Carnegie was persuaded by Walter Damrosch, the German-born American conductor and composer, to build a music hall in New York as a home for the city's two symphony orchestras and the Oratorio Society. On opening night, 5 May 1891, Damrosch conducted the Symphony Society in playing 'America' and Beethoven's Leonore Overture No. 3. Damrosch then stepped down from the podium as Tchaikovsky stepped up to lead the orchestra in the playing of his *Marche Solennelle*. It was the beginning of a five-day festival which attracted the cream of New York society.

At first known as the 'Music Hall Founded by Andrew Carnegie', it was subsequently changed to the 'Carnegie Hall', as the term 'Music Hall' had different connotations in London. It was discovered that foreign performers were turning down invitations because they thought the hall was intended for cheap variety artists.

The Beatles' first tour of the United States started on 7 February 1964. On the 9th they appeared on *The Ed Sullivan Show*, on the 11th they played their first US concert at the Washington Coliseum and the following day they performed at the Carnegie Hall. They opened with a Chuck Berry song:

> *You know my temperature's risin'*
> *The jukebox's blowin' a fuse*
> *My heart beatin' rhythm*
> *And my soul keep singing the blues*
> *Roll over Beethoven*
> *And tell Tchaikovsky the news.*[2]

Music was one of Carnegie's passions, along with golf and fishing. It is difficult to guess how he might have reacted to the popular music of the 1960s being played at a venue which bears his name.

Skibo Castle satisfied Carnegie's sporting passions, and with the help of his wife, Louise, it also became a home for music. It was Louise who hired an organist to greet them with Beethoven's Fifth as they stepped over the threshold of their new home. The organist became a permanent institution:

 Every morning we come down to breakfast greeted by swelling tones, beginning with a hymn or chorale, and swelling into selections from the oratorios, etc. In the evening our musician plays for us on our fine Bechstein piano ...[3]

It would seem that castle guests had no hope of lying abed. In addition to the swelling tones of the organ, a lone piper would circle the main house before *sweeping through the downstairs hall, assuring that all were awake and primed for breakfast, and then returning at dusk to 'pipe' the guests to dinner*.[4]

As well as revelling in her role as the sadistic host, Louise Whitfield Carnegie also played golf.

The Bonar Bridge, Ardgay clubhouse has a tempting view down the first fairway, but a clumsy drive at the tee will be visible to all at the bar—always a sobering consideration for the uninitiated visitor. Erected in 1989, it replaced the original wooden structure that had stood on the same spot since it was built by local joiner, Hugh Ross, in 1907.

The 354-yard first is ominously named *Road Hole* but is significantly less intimidating than its more famous counterpart, there being no intruding hotel or tarmac through the green for the over-exuberant approach shot. Instead, the Bonar Bridge, Ardgay version runs arrow straight and parallel to the Migdale Road before reaching a green protected by bunkers left and right. The joy of this, and many other holes on the course, is the glorious backdrop provided by Loch Migdale and Creag a' Bhealaich. It is a fine setting for a golf course. On the bright April day I played this first hole, I was delighted to open with a par. Combined with the wonderful setting, this was *the* perfect recipe for love at first sight.

And so it continued at the second, the 297-yard, downhill *Wee Burn*. Narrowly avoiding the said burn with a second shot 9-iron, the ball rolled down the green for an easy two-putt. Normally, I would not mention my score, as other people's good fortune on a golf course is rarely a cause for celebration; indeed, it can be downright irritating. My excuse is symmetry; I scored

4s at every hole, including the par 3s, so not so clever after all. The one exception was the par 5, which I will come to later. There is another point to this unnecessary detail, and it is this: with modern equipment, drivers the size of barn doors, it is possible for even the most mediocre hacker, such as me, to turn up at a new course and post a respectable score. Compare this to the skill required to wield clubs from the early 1900s, and you will appreciate the quality of the club's inaugural tee shot on 24 September 1904. The club formally opened as the guest of honour *most deliberately drove off the first ball from the tee, which was a capital shot, being a drive of 96 yards. (Northern Times*, 29 September 1904)

A capital shot indeed. The guest of honour was a lady, obliged to successfully drive the ball in front of an expectant crowd while inevitably suffering from a dose of the early morning bagpipes—it was Louise Whitfield Carnegie.

After the official opening, three of the visiting players from Dornoch—John Sutherland, Walter Matheson and Donald Grant—gave a golfing demonstration. Although not attributed in the club's history, the introduction to *Golf Causerie* states that *Sutherland's close relationship with Mr and Mrs Carnegie played a role in his assistance with the development of the Bonar Bridge, Ardgay Golf Club.*

The course owes its existence to match funding. Andrew Carnegie, an enthusiastic advocate of 'helping those who help themselves', doubled the sum collected from the local populace to enable the course to be constructed on land owned by the Skibo Estate, to the north of the Sutherland Combination

Poorhouse—latterly Migdale Hospital, until its closure in 2011. The course, then and now, occupies the historic Bonar Stance, *where the hardie drovers of more than a century ago rested their 'beasties' overnight on their way to Falkirk tryst in the south.*[5]

Consequently, the grand opening was attended by both Mr and Mrs Carnegie, their daughter, Margaret, and an entourage from Skibo Castle. In advance of Mrs Carnegie's 'capital shot', there was much goodly speech-making, merriment and exchange of gifts, not least an Auchterlonie-manufactured wooden putter for Louise. The formal proceedings were rounded off by Andrew Carnegie, who made a stout defence of the 9-hole layout:

> *The Bonar Club have done the right thing, and they have the correct course, for a 9-hole course is the correct thing, and I will prove it to you. His Majesty the King has a 9-hole course in Windsor, and there is a 9-hole course at Skibo, and when the King and Mr Carnegie have a 9-hole course only, it shows it is the right thing. (Northern Times, 29 September 1904)*

This suggests that Andrew was not beyond some judicious name-dropping; as all the attendees must have been aware, he could count Edward VII among his influential acquaintances, the King having visited Skibo Castle in October 1902, only two years previously. The surprise visit had the musical staff in a panic. *The piper had barely time to get into his garb, and the organist, who had been in the swimming pool, just managed to scramble into his clothes and strike up 'God Save the King' as the royal guest appeared.*[6] *Why should royalty be spared?* was presumably Mrs Carnegie's thinking.

The purpose of the royal visit was to examine the electric lighting and indoor plumbing, as the king, following his accession to the throne in 1901, was wasting no time in remodelling Buckingham Palace. In the same year, he had also established The Royal Household Golf Club in a private section of Windsor Great Park, immediately behind the castle. This is the course referred to in Andrew's speech, and they must surely have discussed and compared. A royal game might even have followed on the Skibo course, but history does not record such an event. Perhaps the king, with a 48-inch waistline, was not best suited to the game and suffered the same handicap as the 25-stone president, William Howard Taft (1909–1913): if he put a ball where he could hit it, he couldn't see it, and if he put a ball where he could see it, he couldn't hit it. The image[7] of dapper Carnegie on the links demonstrates that he would suffer no such problems.

Despite his excesses, Edward VII was a popular royal, and there was a genuine outpouring of national grief when, after a series of heart attacks at Sandringham, he died on 6 May 1910. He lay in state at Westminster Hall until his funeral on 20 May. My Great Uncle Charlie, who worked below stairs at a variety of grand houses at the turn of the century, received these words by postcard from one of his fellow servants:

> *Miss A and I saw the lying in state of the poor king at Westminster Hall, and Miss M gave us a lovely seat and saw the funeral procession. It was a lovely day and such a sight I shall never forget. I was sorry you could not stop and see it.*

Andrew Carnegie would die nine years later, and Louise, more than twenty years his junior, would die at the age of eighty-nine. They are both buried in Sleepy Hollow Cemetery, New York, beneath a Celtic cross.

The third, *Pond*, encapsulates everything that delights about the course: the elevated tee, the closely cropped purple heather, birch, the tall pines, the glimpses of Loch Migdale and the towering Creag a' Bhealaich. The 171-yard green is an inviting iron shot into what feels like an amphitheatre. I could hit balls into this green all day, assuming not too many are lost to the pond to the rear and right of the green. This is followed by *Migdale*, the par 4 fourth, another inviting straight drive between towering pines.

A short walk through the woods from the fourth green brings you to the fifth tee and a fine par 5, rated the hardest hole on the course. A dog-leg left, it demands an accurate and relatively long drive off the tee, such that the pin is visible and your second shot can climb the rising fairway. As everything tends to leak right from the tee, holding the fairway is no easy task. The second shot can also feel tight, as the heather encroaches on both sides and, again, a slope encourages the ball to investigate the rough to your right. One of the more frustrating aspects of golf is when you successfully negotiate the hard shots and then in a moment of relaxed elation mess up the easy ones; my third, a relatively straightforward pitch came up short and bounced into deep rough. The fact that I still rate this hole very highly speaks volumes.

A fine hole this may be, but at this point you are not playing the original layout. Like so many golf courses built in the early 1900s, it has had a chequered history, although it is, at least, based at its original location; my home course, Allendale, has had four quite different homes since being established in 1906.

When first established, the Bonar Bridge, Ardgay course measured 2,107 yards, with none of the holes measuring over 300 yards. By 1935 there had been some significant changes, but it still only measured 2,148 yards, with the first stretched to 312 yards. Although the club survived the Great War and flourished in the 1920s, a lack of members and volunteers following the Second World War ultimately led to its closure in the early 1950s. During this period, the land that comprised the 'triangle', holes seven through nine to the rear of the clubhouse, was sold to the local education authority and converted into a playing field.

The loss of land and the return of unconstrained nature to the entire course, which included hundreds of trees growing on the old fifth and sixth fairways, meant that the committee established in 1966 to resurrect the club faced an enormous challenge. Nevertheless, with significant community effort, the course reopened in 1969 with six holes, extending to nine in 1972. *Last Saturday was a day of sunshine and soft winds, when golfers and friends assembled on the hillside like a Creich Sacrament time of old, but here it was to welcome and celebrate the opening of the 1972 9-hole golf course of the Bonar Bridge, Ardgay Golf Club.*[5]

Beyond this, three further major developments completed the new dawn.

In order to achieve security of tenure, and thereby gain access to grant aid, a direct approach to Andrew Carnegie's daughter, Mrs Carnegie-Miller, led to the purchase of the golf course from the Skibo Estate for £3,000—a transaction completed in December 1980. This in turn opened the doors to local authority and development grants which eventually resulted in the construction and opening of the new clubhouse in 1989. Three years later, Skibo Estate gave the option to purchase a further 140 acres of clear-felled land immediately adjoining the existing course. While this would have been enough to extend to eighteen holes, the more affordable option of lengthening the existing nine was adopted, and so the new third and fourth and the glorious fifth came into being. The construction costs for nine additional holes and, perhaps more significantly, the ongoing maintenance overheads, suggests that this was a wise decision for an off-the-beaten-track, rural club with a small local population and limited opportunities to expand—better to offer something affordable, well presented and different than try to compete with nearby Dornoch, Golspie, et al. Perhaps Andrew's observations came echoing down the years—*when the king and Mr Carnegie have a 9-hole course only, it shows it is the right thing.*

The fully extended course, now 2,581 yards, was opened on 10 April 1998.

The last four holes return to the boundaries of the original course. The sixth, aptly named *Pines*, is another inviting downhill par 3, although much tighter and therefore more testing than the third. The tree-lined seventh, *Tulloch View*, climbs towards an elevated green before progressing to the stroke index 17/18 short par 3, *Wee Bunker*. One assumes this is not an invitation.

Finally, the 311-yard par 4, *Dyke*, takes you home to the clubhouse and the Free Presbyterian Church of Scotland, which overlooks the course. Presumably, golf on a Sunday is no longer considered a sin in this part of Scotland, but even in quite recent times the minister might have been keeping an eye out for transgressors at the first. The club's centenary celebration booklet tells this story from 1969, when the course had recently reopened:

> *... one Sunday James Coghill decided to play and had a pleasant uninterrupted round. He again set out to play on the following Sunday but found his progress stopped on the first fairway by the local minister who informed him that he should not play golf on the Sabbath, whereupon James asked if the minister enjoyed what he did on a Sunday. The minister replied that he very much enjoyed what he did, to which James responded, "Well so do I" and proceeded with his golf. From then on golf was played on Sundays without interruption.*

Notes

1.   'Fourth Time Around', from the 1966 album *Blonde on Blonde* (side 3, track 4). It is believed to be either a parody or homage to The Beatles' 'Norwegian Wood', as they share a similar melody and lyrical premise.

2.   The Beatles' version of Chuck Berry's 'Roll Over Beethoven' was recorded in 1963 and appears on their second LP, *With the Beatles*. Berry's version was originally released as a single by Chess Records in May 1956.

3.   A quote from *Louise Whitfield Carnegie: The Life of Mrs Andrew Carnegie* by Burton Hendrick and Daniel Henderson.

4.   From David Nasaw's *Andrew Carnegie*, Chapter 29, 'We Now Want to Take Root 1897–1898'.

5.   Donald Grant, MA, FRGS, writing in the *Northern Times* in 1972. This is the same Donald Grant who sixty-eight years earlier had provided a golfing demonstration at the opening ceremony together with John Sutherland and Walter Matheson.

6.   From Burton Hendrick's *The Life of Andrew Carnegie*, first published in 1932.

7.   Permission to reproduce this image was kindly given by the Historylinks Museum, Dornoch—www.historylinks.org.uk.

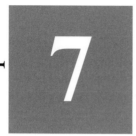

Chapter

Portmahomack

*The wren is a small bird, how
pretty she sings. She bested the
eagle when she hid in its wings.*
Lankum[1]

The eponymous bridge at Bonar Bridge denotes the
boundary between the upstream Kyle of Sutherland and
the downstream Dornoch Firth. Heading south towards
Ardgay, the Kyle is to your right and the Firth to your left. The
A686 road tracks south-east, keeping close company with the Firth
and the railway, the latter after its 25-mile inland detour to Lairg.

Leaving the joys of Bonar Bridge, Ardgay golf course behind, it is
sad to reflect that the club never achieved its royal charter as
Andrew Carnegie proposed at the opening ceremony; he was *sure*

His Majesty would readily grant it. Perhaps the king had weightier matters to occupy him, or maybe the club never got around to asking. It is a shame, as 'Royal Bonar Bridge, Ardgay' has a certain ring to it. Time flies, and opportunities not seized are too easily missed; it was probably their best and only chance. Who else but Carnegie would have the golfing king's ear?

Edward Prince of Wales, as he was at the time, was reportedly introduced to the game in 1859 by his governor, General Robert Bruce, a member of The Royal and Ancient Golf Club of St Andrews (R&A) since 1834. Inspired by an exhibition match at Musselburgh, in 1861 his military association with the Grenadier Guards would take him to Curragh, Ireland, where the recently opened golf course was immediately adjacent to the camp. It is not documented if the future king found time for golf during his ten-week visit, but his extramural activities became infamous. A sexual novice, his fellow guards arranged an introduction to Nellie Clifden, a local 'actress' and possibly a Wren of the Curragh[2] who *knew her way round the camp in the dark*. The resulting affair soon became public knowledge as the guards' tongues wagged, and Nellie became known as the 'Princess of Wales'. The scandal enraged his parents—Queen Victoria and her husband, Prince Albert—and steps were immediately taken to end the liaison. Prince Albert would die a few months later, a demise that Victoria blamed entirely on the anguish caused by Edward's indiscretions—"I never can or shall look at him [Edward] without a shudder."[3] The older generation should never interfere with youthful passion; the ghosts of forbidden fruit can haunt an entire life. If anything is to be learned from this story, it is this: when tempted by sins of the flesh, play more golf.

Victoria's third son was, by contrast, her most cherished. A military man throughout his life—between 1900 and 1904 as Field Marshall HRH The Duke of Connaught—he was appointed commander-in-chief, Ireland. During this time, he played a round at The Curragh with a once-prominent journalist, Lionel Hewson. At one stage Hewson played his ball to within 6 inches of the hole, while the Duke's lay some 10 yards distant. At this point the Duke, exercising the royal prerogative, picked up his ball and remarked, "I always count two on greens, and thus avoid putting."[4] As I seldom single-putt and regularly take three, this is a strategy worthy of contemplation. On balance, I think my putting average would improve.

South of Cambuscurrie Bay, the Ness of Portnacutter and the old ferry point, the A836 joins the A9 and heads south-east with the Far North Line. At a junction 2 miles south, signposted left to Tain and Morangie Road, the B9174 weaves through Tain. One hundred yards beyond the Murray Monument in Tain High Street, the straight-on minor road is signposted *Portmahomack*, a road that will eventually terminate at Tarbat Ness Lighthouse. While the route through the town entirely misses the golf course, the railway is adjacent to some of the fairways—a tempting diversion for the rail passenger, but this journey is heading for a different location.

A remarkably flat landscape for much of the road towards the tip of the peninsula, the terrain is ideal for building aerodromes. More than seventy years after the end of the Second World War, there is much evidence of the decaying infrastructure that supported RAF Tain. Beyond the abandoned airstrips, the Morrich More bombing range occupies an extensive area bordering the Firth and remains in service. This area is also prime farmland, more reminiscent of the Great Plains than a land steeped in ancient Pictish history. There are the inevitable too-yellow fields of oil seed rape, but also many acres given over to potato crops, much of which end up in crackly packets of Walkers Crisps.

Portmahomack is reached after 7 miles. On the approach to the town the road forks left to the seafront and right to the golf course. On 5 October 1899, Mr and Mrs Carnegie visited Portmahomack in their yacht, *Seabreeze*, to address the assembled locals, bury a time capsule and lay the foundation stone of the partially built Carnegie Hall. His attire for such journeys, by road or sea, is well documented: *On cold days butlers and friends would bundle the little figure in a heavy coat, with mufflers, a huge turned-up collar and a hat drawn well over the ears until nothing protruded except nose and goggled eyes; the car would emit a honk, and off the gay party would whirl ...*[5] A pitch-perfect description of A. A. Milne's Toad.

Even by the standards of the late nineteenth century, Carnegie must have seemed a strange cove. A small man with an undoubted talent for making big money, he persisted in identifying with the working man. A January 1885 headline in the *New York Times* proclaimed him the *Millionaire Socialist*. His actions would suggest otherwise.

In order to maximise efficiency, he introduced twelve-hour shifts at his factories, tied wages to the market value of steel and, in 1892, employed armed security agents to enforce lockouts and establish a union-free workplace. The Homestead steel strike, which began on 1 July 1892, was one of the most violent disputes in the history of American private enterprise.

Carnegie's brand of socialism was based on minimum labour costs and maximum profits, in order to support his philanthropic endeavours; in short, he knew better how to spend money than his workers did. His objective was to give away his fortune by the time of his death and establish world peace through arbitration; he singularly failed on all counts. The small man had big ideas, strong opinions and significant influence, derived from wealth. Dinner parties at Skibo must have been intolerable. A romantic and a self-deceiving idealist, his romanticism did not extend to his personal life, finding it impossible to marry his eternally patient Louise until after the demise of his mother. Perhaps his erotic analogies maintained her interest and excitement throughout the long wait. *Louise, you are like Pittsburgh iron—it is very hard to heat at first, but once hot, it is very, very hot indeed and retains its heat extraordinarily.*[6] Could any woman resist? *Remember when our songs were just like prayers, like gospel hymns that you called in the air?*[7]

Drive along the seafront, and at the slight bend in the road, directly opposite the red phone box, turn right into Well Street, and you will be following in the footsteps of the Carnegies, who returned on 16 June 1900 to open the completed hall. Fundraising by the villagers had raised a quarter of the total £800 building cost for the hall, a significant sum in the early 1900s. Carnegie was duly impressed by the community effort but then chose to observe that he was *only surprised they had asked for so little.*

Above the hall and Well Street, footpaths cut through to Castle Street. Turn right, and 200 yards along the road, next to the old primary school, the Portmahomack Golf Club clubhouse sits conveniently adjacent to the Tarbatness Road—visitors welcome. Given the opportunity, it seems inconceivable that, having concluded his speech, the enthusiastic Carnegie would not have found time for 'Doctor Golf'.

In 1911, at the age of seventy-five, he would write glowingly of golf in the *New York Times*: *Played under the sky ... every breath seems to drive away weakness and disease, securing for us longer terms of happy days ... No doctor like Doctor Golf.* He further explained golf's *power to affect the temper, and especially the tongue. We have only to remain silent to produce unusual results ... men become dearer friends than ever; the oftener they meet on the green, the fonder they become of each other.* Not necessarily, Andrew. Not necessarily.

The current club was not established until 1909, but fifteen years previously the *Ross-shire Journal* had reported on the opening round of a new golf course at Portmahomack, laid out on the 'common' area next to the local primary school, land which now forms part of the existing course. There is no evidence that Carnegie ever played golf at Portmahomack, but it is tempting to believe he did, not least because his friend, John Sutherland, once again, was much involved with the establishment of the 1909 layout.

The one certain connection is that in September 1908 the Carnegie Hall was the location used by a group of gentlemen seeking to form a golf club. An influential bunch, they included two men of the cloth, a doctor, the inspector of the poor/registrar, the local primary school headmaster, the postman, the butcher and a host of tenant farmers. The golfing bug had well and truly arrived in Portmahomack and bitten the great and the good. The appropriately named medical man, Dr Pyle, was elected chairman and a golf course committee duly established.[8]

The initial plan had been to site the course at Balnabruach, an area of land to the north of the Tarbatness Road as it approaches the village. However, Sutherland's report on the proposed location was scathing: *a flat uninteresting stretch of country without a single golfing feature.* Stroll along Balnabruach Road today, and it is easy to understand his criticism. Instead, he recommended the Seafield links above the village—*splendid golfing country with an excellent outlook*—the very same turf that had been selected for the original 1894 course. Sutherland concluded that *upon this stretch of sandy links a capital course could be laid out that would form a genuine attraction for the summer visitor.*

Sutherland's report was based on a visit in April 1909, and on 17 June of the same year, the Reverend Donald Macleod placed a ball on a tee for one Mr Gilroy, who drove the ball away with a fair swiping, and the course was declared open to great cheering. In recognition of his significant contribution, John Sutherland was invited to attend the opening ceremony and duly set the lowest score of the day—69 over eighteen holes. Initially seven holes in length, golf had been firmly established in Portmahomack, and there it has remained ever since. It is indeed splendid golfing country. *Portmahomack would be a most desirable summer retreat for all in search of quiet, fresh and invigorating air and rest.*[9] As true in 1909 as it is today. Writing just a few weeks later, John Sutherland observed that *the pioneers of the Portmahomack golfing movement are at present unfortunately faced with one great difficulty: their ground is too much restricted in area. But grand links lie adjacent, which at the present juncture, it would be worth the greatest effort on the part of the community to acquire.*[9]

Again his advice was followed, and in 1912 the club gained access to additional land to the east, and the course extended to nine holes, with further input from John regarding the layout.

In the 1990s the club acquired a further 12 acres which now accommodates the present-day third, fourth and fifth holes. This is the land that you see before you as you step up to the first tee, conveniently adjacent to the car park and clubhouse.

At 277 yards off the yellows,[10] the first, *Ballone*, is a reasonably gentle introduction, with gorse left and right but a fairway that opens out within easy driving distance. It takes its name from Ballone Castle, which is ever present on the horizon to the south-east on holes one through five. For much of the club's existence, the castle was a gaunt sixteenth-century ruin, but in the 1990s a local couple, Lachie and Annie Stewart, undertook an ambitious restoration project. After many years' effort, the rewards of their remarkable endeavours are plain to see—a fully restored medieval castle which has not only enhanced their lives but also those of the local community, the golf club and the surrounding landscape. A glowing testament to the adage, anything is possible.

The approach shot is over a mound which stretches the full width of the green and hides the target from view. Come up a little too short, and a friendly bounce on the bank will most likely put you plumb-centre for a straightforward two-putt. An uncomplicated, gentle introduction can lead to a lifelong relationship. Portmahomack knows how to win friends and influence.

The slightly elevated tee for the second, *Knockshorty*, is to the left of the first green and takes you 292 yards back to the clubhouse. From this tee you can appreciate exactly where you are in the world. Towards the clubhouse, the Dornoch Firth is clearly visible, while in the opposite direction, towards the castle, the Moray Firth also glistens in the distance. It is an inspiring view from sea to shining sea.

I have played the course three times and on every occasion planted my ball in the left-hand semi-rough about 95 yards out from the green. This is not a 'how to' guide; I am not qualified to instruct.

However, this worked for me—aim for the right-hand bunker, and the ball will kick left, leaving you with a certain two-putt for par. It is a simple game when things go well; a trip to purgatory when they don't.

The scope for things to go badly begins at the third, the hardest hole on the course, *Sandy Banks*, measuring 395 yards. Uphill with out-of-bounds and Golf Course Road to the left, distance is needed from the tee. Middling golfers of my ability will be looking to clear the rise in the fairway with their second, such that the green is visible for the final approach to an elevated green. Pitch to the front of the green, and there is every chance that the ball will kick right and roll, in agonising slow motion, into the front-right bunker. I speak from experience—an unjust reward for a golf shot that appeared majestic in mid flight.

At the fourth, the friendly course resumes. *Ballafaddich* is a short, downhill, par 4 at 218 yards. On the sunny, mid-April afternoons I pitched up, the winter tee was so far forward that I was through the green in one. From the slightly elevated tee, the ball soars into a sky which, with luck, will be blue. As it leaves the face of the club, we take ownership of the ball's flight and will earnestly converse with the inanimate object—*Be right, be right!* or in my case, *Come back! Not there, not there!* Very briefly, we are at one with the ball; it becomes part of who we are. It satisfies an internal desire for escape, flight and speed. Perhaps this is my primary attraction to the game—it would explain my lack of enthusiasm for the art of putting.

I have always had a desire for speed, even the early years on a pushbike were about how fast, not where or how far. Throughout fifty years of car ownership, the same principle has applied. In the right sort of four-wheeled vehicle, you directly connect with it—you become part of the machine—but this in no way compares with life on a motorcycle. John Berger continued riding into his nineties:

> *... except for the protective gear you're wearing, there's nothing between you and the rest of the world. The air and the wind press directly on you. You are in the space through which you are travelling. Your contact with the outside world is more intimate. You're more conscious of the road surface, its subtle variations, its potholes, whether it's dry or damp, of mud or gravel; you're aware of the hold of the tyres, or their lack of it; bends produce another effect: if you enter one properly, it holds you in its arms. A hill points you to the sky. A descent lets you dive into it. Every contour line on the map of the country you are riding through means your axis of balance has changed ... This perception is visual but also tactile and rhythmic. Often your body knows quicker than your mind.[11]*

On four wheels you can become part of the machine. On two wheels you *are* the machine.

I imagine the same man–machine relationship exists between the pilot and the jet fighter; not something I was born to experience, as my enthusiasm for speed vanishes when the machine is not firmly attached to Mother Earth. On any day in the skies above Portmahomack, it is quite possible to see this relationship at work as low-flying aircraft make for the Morrich More bombing range. Their arrival will be perfectly timed to coincide with the top of your backswing.

The distinctive red and white Tarbat Ness Lighthouse forms part of the golf club's logo and is proudly displayed on the road-facing side of the clubhouse. Built by Robert Stevenson at the tip of the peninsula, 3 miles north-east of the golf club, it has been flashing its beacon of light across the dark waters of the Moray Firth since 1830. At 174 feet, it provides a useful navigational aid, and not always for shipping.

The SEPECAT[12] Jaguar was a British–French jet attack aircraft in service with the Royal Air Force and a familiar sight above Portmahomack in the 1970s. At that time, aircraft navigation systems were not as advanced as we might imagine, and finding Morrich More was assisted by Stevenson's maritime creation.

> *... we would fly over the lighthouse to get a fix, the most accurate way to do so, and find the target for the Jaguar. It had an early inertial navigation system which was prone to drift and which needed frequent updates.*

As for that all-important variable, speed:

> *... assuming a direct track of 12 kilometres (6.5 nautical miles) from the lighthouse and a level attack (called laydown) at 8 nautical miles a minute, the time to reach the target would be about forty-nine seconds.[13]*

They were not hanging about.

By the time the Tornado GR1/4 arrived on the scene, navigational systems had much improved, and this device was so noisy that it was frowned upon to fly over the lighthouse or anywhere near. Nevertheless, the locals have got used to all this aerial activity over the years. As the club's 2019 captain, Harry Corbett observes, *this area has a long, long association with the RAF bombing range on Morrich More, going back to World War II days. Locals are well used to jets, bombers and helicopter gunships rattling and bombing away—when you live here, it's part of the scenery. Once a year, at Tain Gala Day, we get a fly-past from the Red Arrows in the Firth—our reward for forbearance.*

The fifth, *Don's View* (named after a volunteer greenkeeper—where would we be without them?) is a 165-yard par 3, and at stroke index 8 is no pushover. Ballone Castle is clear on the horizon, but much more immediate is the out-of-bounds all the way down the left. To the right is some heavy rough, while the approach to the hole is guarded by two bunkers right and left. There is no hiding place; you must hope you are straight and long from the tee. On a still day it just requires competence, but into a strong prevailing westerly, I imagine it an entirely different kettle of fish.

At the sixth, *Seafield*, you play across the full history of the course. Like many courses of long standing, Portmahomack has evolved over time. Modest beginnings, starting with the 7-hole course layout, expanded through a history of rental and finally acquisition to the current 10-hole course. The tee is positioned on the Bindal Land, some of which was not acquired until the 1980s. The fairway traverses the Department Land, and the green is positioned on Glebe Land, links turf that formed part of the original course of 1894 and the 'common' area.

The view from the sixth tee is daunting. Out-of-bounds runs all the way down the left, the fairway is cratered and there is no obvious preferred destination for your drive. My natural tendency to fade/slice from the tee turned out to be the right answer to the challenge of the hardest hole on the course.[14] Anything left will probably drift beyond the white markers, anything down the middle will most likely bounce left towards out-of-bounds while anything right should hold up on the high ground for a blind shot into the green. Protected by bunkers right and left and a boundary wall through the green, par must feel like some achievement. I don't know for sure; I never found out in three attempts.

A few steps from the sixth green, and in front of the equipment shed, is the seventh tee for the aptly name *Bunkers* hole. A blind shot over rising ground, the pin is invisible, as are the bunkers. The short-iron tee shot to the 122-yard par 3 green is an act of blind faith, especially for the unknowing casual visitor.

There was a time when power lines and their supporting poles cut across the course diagonally, with the familiar local rules demanding a free drop if you hit them or another drive if you clipped them off the tee. In my experience at Allendale, the second shot is never as sweetly hit as the first. The removal of the cables and poles in the 1970s allowed a restructuring of the course, and the sixteenth was created to add diversity and a unique claim to be the only 10-hole course on the east coast. More challenging than the blind seventh, *Plateau*, is a 155-yard par 3. The pin may be visible from the elevated tee on a hill to the right of the seventh, but the approach over heavily undulating rough and between two rough-covered mounds demands an accurate, long drive from the tee. There is no escape clause; the green is the only safe destination. The eighth, *Jackie's Brawest*, a 288-yard par 4, is my favourite on the course. Named after Jackie Mackay, a greenkeeper from the 1970s responsible for re-siting the green away from the boundary wall, it is a glorious downhill drive where, seemingly regardless of the direction of travel from the tee, your ball will gather down to a hollow on the right, about 80 yards out from the green. The second shot over a steep bluff is daunting—an elevated green protected by bunkers right and left with a sloping run-off to the rear which will take the over-ambitious to the road beyond.

If truth be told, I had a disturbed upbringing. At some point in the late 1950s the family acquired a record player. A plastic- coated cream box with a red lining and a detachable speaker in the lid. This magical device was designed to play 78 rpm discs, a stack of up to ten 45 rpm discs and single LPs. As the junior family member, I had no say in the initial purchase of records. At that time I probably had no knowledge or opinion on such matters. My sister by contrast was besotted by Pat Boone, and my non-musical parents, for reasons beyond my comprehension, thought *Noel Coward at Las Vegas*, *Oklahoma* and *South Pacific* would be just the thing. No wonder Lennon, McCartney and Zimmerman would come as such blessed relief.

Other than 'Mad Dogs and Englishmen', Coward was beyond my understanding. In the years before the musical revolution of the sixties, I had no choice but to familiarise myself with the crooning of a clean-cut college boy, the music of Richard Rodgers and the lyrics of Oscar Hammerstein II. My favourite track from *South Pacific* was this:

>*Bloody Mary is the girl I love.*
>*Bloody Mary is the girl I love.*
>*Bloody Mary is the girl I love.*
>*Now ain't that too damn bad!*

Expletives in excess of four characters were commonplace in our household, but I was barred from joining in.

> *Mother*: Robin! Stop that swearing immediately!
> *Me*: I'm not; I'm singing!
> *Mother*: I won't tell you again. Stop that now!

But I didn't and she did, usually with painful consequences. I have been using expletives ever since, nowhere more often than on a golf course, and not always adhering to the greater-than-four-letter rule. The approach to the eighth brought them out in abundance. In three attempts I respectively came up short in the bluff, found a bunker and flew the green to the road beyond. *Now ain't that too damn bad!*

The ninth, *School*, takes you home. My shape of drive from the tee requires an act of faith which I am sometimes loath to test. The par 4 327-yard fairway is a mild dog-leg left, such that a fading ball demands a flightpath that starts in the direction of the graveyard on Tarbatness Road. How many bible-black, bowed-head gatherings have been disturbed by golf balls clattering among the headstones.

Once the mourners have been negotiated, the fairway heads slightly to the left again, towards the rear of the school. The area encompassing the graveyard, playing field and school is known as 'Gaza', either because historically it was a sandy area resembling the Gaza desert or because the local minister considered the residents Philistines for their poor church attendance. I prefer the latter explanation. Perhaps they were out on the links perfecting a straight drive. What better way to avoid the perils of deviating from the path of the righteous?

A non-righteous Allendale stalwart who made the pilgrimage to Portmahomack many years ago warned that he had managed to plant a ball into the school playground. *How did he do that?* I smugly wondered, and then promptly put my second shot within 2 feet of the school wall.

On my next round the ball came up short, and on my final attempt I reached the green in regulation. I was at the far right and the pin at the far left. It is a long, narrow green. In my excitement I four-putted. According to the rules of Field Marshall HRH The Duke of Connaught, I parred the last. He was no fool.

Notes

1. From 'Hunting the Wren' by the Irish folk band Lankum. It first appeared on their album, *The Live Long Day*, released on 25 October 2019. The 'wren' is a direct reference to the Wrens of the Curragh.

2. Wrens of the Curragh were an outcast community of nineteenth-century Irish women who lived rough, brutally hard lives on the plains of Kildare. The name comes from the shelters they lived in, hollowed out 'nests' in the ground which they covered with layers of furze. Their number included unmarried mothers, free-thinkers, alcoholics, prostitutes, vagrants, ex-convicts and harvest workers. All of them women who had, in one way or another, put themselves beyond the pale of respectable society. 'Songbirds on Society's Margins', *The Irish Times*, 13 October 2001.

3. Victoria, as quoted in Jane Ridley's *Bertie: A Life of Edward VII.*

4. This story is adapted from *Golf Quarterly* Issue 16, Winter 2014, pages 15–17, 'The Curragh takes the Honour'. This in turn was adapted from Scott Macpherson's *Golf's Royal Clubs Honoured by The British Royal Family 1833–2013.*

5. From Burton Hendrick's, *The Life of Andrew Carnegie*, the text describes a December trip to the Westchester Hills, White Plains, New York, in 1907.

6.   *Andrew Carnegie*, Chapter 16, 'Things Fall Apart, 1886–1887', David Nasaw.

7.   'The Stable Song' from the 2016 album, *Gregory Alan Isakov with the Colorado Symphony*.

8.   Much of the historical golf club information in this chapter is derived from the club's centenary booklet, *Tarbat Golf Club, Portmahomack: The First 100 Years. Centenary 1909–2009*. To avoid confusion when promoting the club, the 'Tarbat' name was replaced by Portmahomack in 2015. Tarbat is an old church parish name and does not appear on any maps.

9.   *Golf Causerie*, page 234, 'Portmahomack: Pioneers' Difficulty', 3 July 1909, John Sutherland.

10. Here, and throughout this book, it is generally safe to assume that yardages are quoted from the yellow tees. Portmahomack operates a white and blue tee system for competition distances: white on the front nine, measuring 2,560 yards, and blue on the back nine, measuring 2,628 yards—a total of 5,188 yards.

11. An extract from John Berger's 'How Fast Does It Go?', one of a collection of essays in his 1992 publication, *Keeping a Rendezvous*.

12. *Société Européenne de Production de l'Avion d'École de Combat et d'Appui Tactique* (The European Company Established for the Production of a Combat Trainer and Tactical Support Aircraft).

13. Quotes from Wing Commander Chris Barker RAF (retd).

14. The sixth is stroke index 4 and 3 on the front nine and back nine respectively. My opinion on the degree of difficulty is supported by the description of the hole in the club's centenary booklet (page 27): *Many consider this to be one of the hardest holes*.

The Black Isle

Everything passes, everything changes, nothing stays the same.
Lizabett Russo[1]

As misleading trade descriptions go, the Black Isle is up there with Cowes, Braintree and Liverpool—it is neither black nor an isle—but despite the misleading sales pitch, this is the next port of call.

There was some regret at leaving Portmahomack. Easily passed by in haste on the A9, it has much to offer. The locals are friendly, as we discovered on our first night; at a Lizabett Russo concert in the Carnegie Hall we were introduced to half of the attendees and offered free drinks. In addition to the fine golf course, there are any number of walks with fascinating destinations, such as Stevenson's Lighthouse, the village of Rockfield and Ballone Castle.

It is an area steeped in ancient history, and the story is well told in the Tarbat Discovery Centre, housed in the old parish church of Saint Colman, just over the boundary wall at the southern end of the golf course. Perhaps, most surprisingly of all, Portmahomack benefits from the most glorious sunsets—it is the only fishing village on the east coast which faces west.

The conventional route to the Black Isle would be down the A9, across the Cromarty Bridge and then left at Tore along the A832, but there is a more direct and far more interesting route via Nigg, but only if you are travelling in the summer months.

The B9165 road heads south out of Portmahomack and leads down towards Fearn. At the Balmuchy crossroads, immediately following the grey warehouses, a sharp left takes you to Hilton of Cadboll and Baltinore. Both once had their own golf courses, while a third was briefly established by RAF officers at the nearby airfield. Everything has passed, although there is still flying activity out of Easter Airfield on the southern side of RAF Fearn, where, in common with Tain, some of the wartime infrastructure remains in place. From 1939 to 1945 this whole peninsula would have been an altogether more active place.

The country lane winds its way south through Blackhill, Pitcalnie and Nigg to the end of the road at Nigg Ferry. It is here, during the summer months, that a small ferryboat crosses to Cromarty and provides a link between the Tarbat Peninsula and the Black Isle. The area immediately adjacent to the ferry landing has also changed out of all recognition. Face north from the jetty, and the land to the left was once dominated by the magnificent Dunskaith House, destroyed by fire in 1960. To the right is the collection of buildings that once formed the Nigg Ferry Hotel and, behind that, the rough ground that served as the golf links, variously known as Castlecraig, Nigg and at one time Cromarty Golf Club. The course has all but disappeared, except for imagined traces of tee boxes, fairways and bunkers—*all that remains of the groundsman's pains for the rest of time and a day.*[2]

The club was originally founded as a private 9-hole course in 1890. Storm-blown sand created what was thought by some to be *the finest natural course in the world.*[3] A description is included in a 1904 edition of *Golf Illustrated* magazine:

> *The course lies along the beach, a magnificent stretch of sand, and is of great variety. There are many natural hazards. The turf is all that can be desired, being in the centre of a large stretch of bent. The greens remain much as they were formed by nature, only raking and rolling being necessary to keep them in excellent condition. Whin, broom and bent are the punishments of erratic players, but the good golfer can appreciate the exceedingly fine pieces of sandy turf. Large natural sand holes await the unwary on every hand.*

The ten-minute ferry from Cromarty, encouraging golfers to cross the water from the Black Isle and visits by the Home Fleet to Invergordon every spring and autumn, meant the course was well patronised to the point of congestion. In October 1908 the proprietor, Colonel Ross, presided over a meeting to discuss possible course extension. Captain Evans of the Dreadnought had suggested *that as it was probable the fleet would often be in the Cromarty Firth during the next few years, it would be a great convenience to the officers that the course be extended to eighteen holes*. With the full weight of naval command behind the proposal, the motion was duly carried. The significant costs would be met by doubling annual subscriptions and *it is expected that the golfing officers will heartily cooperate*. Golf was a game for the senior ranks. There is no mention of access for naval ratings. Press images from the time show sailors in uniform carrying bags for their superiors. They were known as 'tar-caddies'.

The design of the extension was undertaken by Alexander MacHardy, Scotland's forgotten, turn-of-the-century golf architect responsible for laying out a wide variety of Scottish courses across the Highlands (including Lochcarron[4]). The new layout totalled 5,055 yards and is described in detail by Alexander Polson, the Nigg schoolmaster, in his book, *Easter Ross*:

The holes provide plenty of variety, both with regard to length and difficulty. There are two splendid short holes surrounded by natural hazards, a ditch having to be crossed in each case. About eight of the holes may be reached by the long player with two strokes, but for the average player they mean three. Three of the holes are three-shot holes, the others being drive and iron or drive and pitch. The hazards throughout are natural, there being only one or two artificial bunkers.

The Golf Links and Club House, Nigg, (Ross-shire).

The *Ross-shire Journal* reports from 1931 suggest a busy period at the club, with a wide variety of member and open competitions being played for throughout the year. There is no mention of officers or their tar-caddies. Perhaps other events were taking priority.

On 11 September 1931, the Atlantic Fleet, comprising ten warships, arrived at Invergordon, coincident with newspaper reports of large pay cuts for officers and senior and junior ratings. The pay cuts had been introduced by Ramsay MacDonald's National Government in response to the Great Depression. This ill-advised policy resulted in 1,000 sailors going on strike from 15–16 September until the most invasive cuts had been reversed.

The Invergordon Mutiny is almost unique in British military history and had consequences far beyond the shores of the Cromarty Firth. Reports of the naval strike caused a run on the pound, panic on the stock exchange and finally, on 21 September 1931, contributed to Britain being forced off the Gold Standard, leading to a sharp devaluation in sterling. This helped the country recover from the depression but effectively lowered the value of everyone's income. The universal pay cut had been reintroduced by sleight of hand.

> *Everybody knows that the dice are loaded,*
> *Everybody rolls with their fingers crossed,*
> *Everybody knows that the war is over,*
> *Everybody knows the good guys lost.*
> *Everybody knows the fight was fixed,*
> *The poor stay poor; the rich get rich.*[5]

An intriguing coda to this passage of history is the story of the strike leader, Len Wilcott. Three years later he defected to Russia, became embroiled in the Siege of Leningrad, surviving only to be imprisoned in the Gulag for more than ten years, accused of being a British spy. On his release he befriended the traitor, Donald MacLean. In the great golf game of life, Len had a knack for picking some rum playing partners.

According to the sign near Nigg Pier, the Cromarty Ferry runs every half an hour between 08:00 and 18:00 from 1 June to 30 September. At the time of writing, it is operated by Highland Ferries and charges steep fares for a ten-minute crossing—cash only. If this is what it takes for it to survive, then long may it do so. Subject to weather and tides, the ferry will deliver you to Cromarty Harbour, all the while overlooked by a multitude of laid-up oil rigs—black gold and natural gas long ago replaced the navy as the primary occupant of the Firth.

I had not thought death had undone so many.[6]

Cromarty is a tidy place, protected from the worst winter storms by the high ground to the east—the Sutors of Cromarty and Gallow Hill. The town's most famous son is Hugh Miller, the stonemason, geologist, palaeontologist and writer. A deeply religious man, his beliefs were permanently at odds with his scientific endeavours—an internal conflict that may have contributed to his suicide. Hugh shot himself at his Edinburgh home on Christmas Eve 1856. Hugh Miller's birthplace celebrates his life; a humble thatched cottage on Church Street stands adjacent to a fine Georgian building which houses the Hugh Miller Museum. Beyond this is the Cromarty Court House Museum and next to this the Hugh Miller Institute, a rather too grandiose building for its setting, funded by the Andrew Carnegie Trust and opened in 1904. Above the door are inscribed the words *Meane Weil, Speak Weil and Doe Weil*. Consequently, I will say no more on the diminutive chap, Carnegie.

The main road out of Cromarty, the A832, heads south-west through fertile Black Isle fields, arriving at Rosemarkie and the coast within 10 miles. Through the village and north of Fortrose, a left turn off Ness Road, signposted *Chanonry Point*, leads down to the lighthouse and a shoreline dotted with cockeyed optimists staring intently out to sea, searching for dolphins. This is the road that cuts through the Fortrose & Rosemarkie golf course, hallowed undulating turf that has played host to golf since 1793.

By rights this course should not be included in this journey. I have already strayed from 9-hole courses, but this busy links with eighteen holes and no honesty box was too tempting to pass by. A friendly professional halved the green fee as I was nearing twilight time. I was immediately well disposed to the place. It is a fine stretch of links with arresting views from tee to green on every hole. For the casual visitor it is difficult to pick out one special hole; they all are. It is a reassuring coincidence that while the French Revolution's Reign of Terror was in full swing, the British were building golf courses. As the French honed their guillotines to slice the gentry, we were commandeering the links to slice golf balls. This significant date is carved into the bank of the eighteenth tee, fully visible from the clubhouse and styled in the manner of the Fovant Badges. The club proudly claims to be the fifteenth oldest golf course in the world; it is surprising there are so many which are even older.

From the road, the course appears to occupy a narrow strip of land between the town and the lighthouse, but there is ample space on both sides, and only the wildest of drives is likely to attack passing traffic.

The exceptions are the fifth, a short par 3 at the top of the course that crosses the road, and the slightly daunting twelfth and thirteenth, where the narrow fairway is bordered by heavy gorse on the right and the road on the left.

At the thirteenth my drive crossed the road for a subsequent blind 9-iron, over gorse in full bloom, onto the edge of the green. It was one of the few holes I parred on the back nine—my game is much improved by blind faith. The back of the fourteenth green is denoted by large white painted boulders—a strong hint not to go too long, otherwise vehicular contact is more than likely.

For all its remarkable vistas, it is the fourth and fifth at the top end of the course, nearest the lighthouse, that leave the most enduring impression; a shame, in some respects, that they come so early in the round. The signature hole, the fourth, *Lighthouse*, looks innocuous from the tee (stroke index 1, par 5 off the whites and par 4 off the yellows). Those of us middling golfers who reach for the driver, seeking distance under all circumstances, will be in for a sad surprise. The marker post may offer an idealised line for the competent, but it also coincides with a deep dip in the fairway and some unpleasant rough to the right. I got lucky, landed on an elevated path, took a drop from knee height, of course, and then found myself with an inviting long pitch to the green. Anything long into the green and you are faced with a knee-trembling downhill putt, while anything short is likely to roll off the front and into a severe dip. I threatened the pin, briefly, and then watched in despair as the ball rolled some distance off the green. I was moderately happy to walk off with a 6—I am not an ambitious golfer. The lighthouse provides the perfect backdrop throughout. Designed by Alan Stevenson, it first came into service in 1846 and adjoins a collection of Egyptian-styled keepers' cottages.

To the right of the fourth green can be seen the tees for the fifth, a short par 3, *Icehouse*, which crosses the road and any traffic entering or leaving the Chanonry Point car park. The hardest hole on the course is followed by one of the 'easiest', at stroke index 17. There is rough almost all the way to the green, where the putting surface cosies up to the road, and at the back there is the beautiful briny sea. To the left are a collection of buildings which include the ferry house—once an inn and home to the ferryman who plied the waters between Chanonry Point and Fort George. A passenger ferry operated until 1953. I found the fifth green in one with a 'perfectly' executed pitching wedge—the subsequent three-putt was not so cleverly executed. It was from the sixth that the pace of life turned glacial.

I can be reasonably certain that this was the first photograph I ever took. It is in the back garden in Hale, Altrincham, and I would be using the only camera the family owned for years: the 120-roll film, Kodak Brownie Cresta.

"Be careful", "Don't drop it", "Press the shutter once" and "Don't forget to wind it on" would have been just a selection of the instructions received from my ever-vigilant mother. In perfect nosey-neighbour fashion, Mrs Hillier is watching proceedings from an upper window. She would have felt much at home in the Stasi.

The trellis fence in the background divided east from west and would take my weight for all the years it was necessary. Retrieval of footballs, tennis balls, paper aeroplanes and cricket stumps/harpoons was a constant necessity and inevitably resulted in shouted orders from either side of the divide. Children in the

1950s were at best tolerated, always mistrusted and invariably harshly punished. We knew our place.

The Stasi, Mrs Hillier, was married to an ex-RAF officer, 'affectionately' known as 'Hillybum'—I have no idea why. He drove a cream Mk VIII Hillman Minx at a time when all cars were black. The connection between Hillman, Hillier and Hillybum was reassuringly alliterative—entirely logical.

He would pass away not long after this was taken, but not before we all ended up on the same beach in Wales one bright summer. This was entirely by coincidence, happy or otherwise. The gathering from left to right comprises Mrs Hillier (taking notes), their daughter Joy (eternally single), me (performing cat impressions), sister Pat (eating, as always), mother (presiding over the sandwich tin), Hillybum, Cousin Brian, Uncle Ed and Aunt Bet:

Analogue photography is self-regulating. The price and limited exposures available on roll film kept the finger away from the shutter. The anxious wait while the exposed film was sent away for processing meant the pictures were fewer, the decisive moments more significant. Despite this limitation, the one constant throughout my life is that I have always had access to a camera and, for a large part of that time, until the advent of digital, access to a darkroom. I have taken an enormous number of photographs.

Under almost all circumstances I will carry a Fuji X100[7] 23 mm fixed-lens camera in my golf bag, a device that emulates the look and feel of the Olympus Pen F and Leica M series. The number of images I take depends on the views from the course and the pace of play.

At Fortrose & Rosemarkie I could have filled a memory card. There are certainly show-stopping views from every tee, but camera time became extensive because of the six-ball in front—four players of mixed ability, an itinerant wife and a bored dog. It was the perfect reminder of why the empty fairways of 9-hole courses are such an attraction. In fairness to the four players, wife and dog, we were finally invited to play through—at the seventeenth. I declined. At heart I am a curmudgeon.

Notes

1.	From the Lizabett Russo track, 'Times of Change', self-published in 2017. Originally from Brasov in Transylvania, she combines Eastern European, World and Celtic music in a unique style of delivery. Sadly under-appreciated on the Tarbat Ness peninsula, there were only sixteen attendees at her 2019 appearance at Portmahomack.

2.	Adapted from Roy Harper's 'When an Old Cricketer Leaves the Crease', which appears on his 1975 album, *HQ*.

3.	*Nigg: A Changing Parish* by Anne Gordon, Chapter 29, 'The Castlecraig (Nigg) Golf Club'.

4.	Lochcarron, a short 9-hole course that straddles the A896, is featured in the first *Golf in the Wild* book, Chapter 8.

5.	'Everybody Knows', written by Leonard Cohen in collaboration with Sharon Robinson. It was first released on his *I'm Your Man* album in February 1988.

6.	From Dante's 'Inferno'/T. S. Eliot's 'The Burial of the Dead'.

7.	The type of X100 is deliberately omitted. Having started with the X100S, this was swapped for the X100F, and at the time of writing, the intention is to upgrade to the X100V.

Chapter 9

Moray Coast

She misses her footing on the social ladder at least three times a week. Mervyn Peake[1]

ort George is visible across the Moray Firth from Chanonry Point and much of the Fortrose & Rosemarkie golf course. Built in the eighteenth century in response to the Jacobite uprising, it is the largest artillery fortification in the UK by some margin. The site is home to the Highlanders' Museum, and much of it is now open to the public. Although still an operational barracks, in 2016 the Ministry of Defence announced that it would close in 2032.

To the east of the fort, and beyond the rifle ranges, the 9-hole Ardersier golf course once provided a distraction for officers and

124

gentlemen. The club was not long lived, opening in 1908 and closing in the late 1920s. The *Northern Chronicle* of July 1908 described the course: ... *which is an undulating one, skirts the common at Fort George and overlooks the Firth at different points. It possesses quite a number of natural hazards. A few of the greens are somewhat small, but these can be easily extended.*

In the early summer of 1914, Lieutenant Fred Ricketts, a member of the 2nd Battalion of the Argylls, and its army band were stationed at Fort George. An occasional golfer, Fred was playing Ardersier one bright morning when a sharp two-note whistle rang out across the course, swiftly followed by a wayward golf ball. The tuneful hacker had whistled B flat and G instead of shouting "Fore!". According to Fred's wife Annie, writing in 1958, the two-note warning *with impish spontaneity was answered by my husband with the next few notes. There was little sauntering— Moray Firth's stiff breezes encouraged a good crisp stride. These little scraps of whistling appeared to 'catch on' with the golfers, and from that beginning, the 'Quick March' was built up.* Frederick Joseph Ricketts was better known by his publishing name, Kenneth J. Alford, the renowned composer of marching-band music. The short refrain that began on the banks of the Moray Firth in the days immediately preceding the Great War would become one of the most instantly recognisable pieces of band music ever written—the appropriately named 'Colonel Bogey March'. The connection with the golf scoring term is not coincidental.

At its narrowest point, the crossing between Chanonry Point and Fort George on the Moray Coast is less than three quarters of a mile. The passenger ferry across the Firth encouraged the occasional match between Ardersier and Fortrose & Rosemarkie; enthusiastic bands of plus-four besuited players would regularly wobble aboard the small boat, golf bags sat upright like oars at rest. The demise of the ferry must have been an inconvenience for more than the golfing fraternity, especially in the years preceding the building of the Kessock Bridge, north of Inverness.

The route down to Inverness and east along A96 takes you to Nairn, the first major town along the Moray Coast, 8 miles as the crow flies from Chanonry Point—just short of thirty by modern-day roads. The route passes Inverness Airport and the very grand Castle Stuart Golf Links, which has played host to the Scottish Open. The most northerly of venues for this tournament, the Highland weather wreaked havoc in 2011 when torrential rain caused landslips on holes one and twelve. The adverse conditions had no lasting impact, the tournament returning on three subsequent occasions.

Beyond Nairn, the A96 heads for Forres, tracking the old Inverness and Aberdeen Junction Railway for much of the way—a line that survived Beeching and remains in use. At the Findhorn Roundabout, a sharp left takes you to Kinloss along the B9011, where it becomes the B9089 at the Abbey Inn junction and heads further east. The 11-hole Kinloss Country Golf Club is passed on the right. A rise in the road level just before Roseisle Maltings is evidence that you are crossing the now-abandoned Burghead Branch Line, and almost immediately following, a junction is signposted left—*Burghead, 2.5 miles*. Before entering the town, a right turn to Lossiemouth along the B9040 leads to Cummingston and Hopeman before arriving at the small hamlet of Covesea. A few white houses facing the road from the north are the only evidence of Wester Covesea, while beyond the crossroads a collection of farm buildings on the left indicates Easter Covesea. A few yards beyond that, a track to the left is signposted *Covesea*

Golf Links. The unmade road drops to the shoreline and one of the most remarkable 9-hole layouts in the country. At the western end of Covesea Links, under the perpetual gaze of Alan Stevenson's lighthouse, Andy Burnett has created golfing magic.

John B. Sheridan, writing in the early twentieth century, observed that:

> *Any pleasure there is in golf comes from hitting the ball, but as soon as you begin to hit it regularly and with skill, you come up against the astounding contradiction that the whole aim is to hit the ball as seldom as possible. The better you play, the less you play. The more you play, the worse you are. In fact, as golf gets better, it tends to eliminate itself!*

Sheridan was being deliberately obtuse. As any first-rate hacker will know, the pleasure of striking one good ball into a distant green or sinking a 15-foot putt is worth any amount of golfing mediocrity. Indeed, it is for these rare and bright moments that the average golfer will keep turning out. Less in golf is more.

John B., or 'Sherry' to his many avid readers, was a successful Irish–American sportswriter who would eventually hang himself by his dressing gown cord at the age of sixty-one. He should have spent more time on the links, where life's worries are guaranteed to be put in perspective. He should have gone to Covesea.

There is one problem with this recommendation: despite appearances, the golf course was only established in 2010. Built around natural features, high ground, cliff faces, enormous rocks and ideal links land, it is remarkable.

Andy Burnett bought the land about fifteen years ago and, with his brother Graeme, expended huge effort in turning it into a 9-hole golf course ... *as soon as I saw the place, I fell in love with it completely.*[3]

Unusually, Covesea is not a members' club, so the course is entirely Andy's domain, thereby avoiding the plague of the grumpy golfer who will seek to blame all his misfortune on

128

anything but his inadequate game. Consequently, the usual rules, regulations and members' priority are entirely missing. "We've always run the place without any airs and graces—everyone is welcome to come and play."[3] It is an operational model that I find extremely attractive.

The course opens with a 207-yard par 3 which demands an accurate drive to the green against the prevailing winds. At only stroke index 8/17, I have nevertheless always found it a tough opener. Anything over 150 yards demands a degree of driving accuracy that I do not possess with longer clubs.

The next three par 4s play out across relatively flat links land, culminating in the very fine stroke index 1 fourth which follows the curve of the bay. There is the constant sound of the sea, fine-sanded bunkers, rocky outcrops, drainage ditches and marram grass waiting to ensnare the wayward golf ball. Set on well-drained links turf, it is land that first inspired men to hit balls with ill-designed sticks. To cap it all, the greens are first class. The occasional low-flying jet out of RAF Lossiemouth will disturb the peace, probably at the height of your backswing.

While the first four holes are great entertainment and provide a classic links golf experience, it is at the fifth that the genius of Covesea is revealed. A blind par 3 at 90 yards, a short-iron must deliver the ball 33 feet above to a narrow banana-shaped green sitting at the high point of the course. The views down the coast and towards the lighthouse demand to be savoured before sinking that elegant birdie 2. The image below is from the fifth green, and remarkably this is my blind tee shot. Yes, even more remarkably, I sank the putt!

Golf in the Wild

Regardless of hitting strength, the sixth, another par 3, is driveable at 221 yards because the tee is so elevated that the ball is immediately launched Apollo-like into the yonder blue. At this distance, and from this height, finding a safe landing is akin to piloting the *Eagle* into the Sea of Tranquility. The golfing landscape painter and poet, Frederick Partridge (1849–1929) would surely have enjoyed Covesea, armed with pen, brush or club:

> *Who sweeps neatly from the tee,*
> *And starts me flying far and free,*
> *Filled to the core with silent glee?*
> *My driver.*[4]

As if this were not enough fun, the seventh is a blind par 3 to an elevated tee, demanding a 135-yard carry over a 14-foot, gorse-covered, rocky outcrop. Walking around this natural obstacle to find your ball laying *content, two paces from the pin*[5] is immensely rewarding—I imagine.

Above the seventh green, the eighth tee is tucked into the cliff face, and the ball must be driven between the rocky outcrop on the left and more high ground on the right; there is every chance the ball will again disappear. At 232 yards, this relatively short par 4 is nevertheless a true test of golf, enhanced by a large bunker to the right of an offset green. Above the eighth green, a short climb takes you to the ninth tee, cut into another cliff face.

The finishing hole is a wonder or a stinker; the result of your tee shot will determine your point of view. At 104 yards it looks straightforward, but your exit from the tee is tightly protected to the right by gorse and rocks, and the miniature green is the shape of an upturned porridge bowl; anything not dead centre will kick off in a random direction. In four attempts, I got it right once, using a sand wedge when the tees were well forward and the hole shortened by some 10 yards. It is a great finish to an excellent and unique nine holes. If I lived nearer, I would be at Covesea every week.

A credit to Andy Burnett, the only facility lacking at the time of writing is a clubhouse. Sadly, the original Tee Shack was destroyed by fire in 2014, a blaze which thirty-five firefighters took more than two hours to control. The fire had a devastating impact on visitor numbers, as the Tee Shack's popularity reached beyond the golfing fraternity. In the immediate aftermath there was concern for the ongoing viability of the course. It is reassuring that many years on, this wonderful course continues to survive.

You can determine much about a golf course from its clubhouse. Except for Fortrose & Rosemarkie, all the clubhouses visited in this and the previous book are a world away from the plush surroundings of a well-heeled 18-hole course and on a different planet from anything to be found at, or near, St Andrews.

There are many styles of clubhouse to be found on the *Golf in the Wild* journey, but I remember Strathtay, in the heart of Highland Perthshire, as typical of the atmosphere at many small clubs across Scotland, from the Borders to the far north. The clubhouse is approached across the first and ninth fairways (there is no paved access) and gives the impression of a building that dates from the birth of the course. It may have been through several upgrades, but the atmosphere is tied to a distant past. Pine panelled and slightly musty, the walls are adorned with photographs of former glories, competition details, handicap lists and rather too many instructions from the committee. All important stuff, but dutifully ignored by the members who always have weightier matters to consider: *Have I packed a banana?* or *Will I finally par the fourth?*

From recollection, the Strathtay building is unique in that it combines an equipment shed with the main clubhouse. An elevated verandah to the front is optimistically populated with seating for those rare occasions when the sun shines and the midges don't drive everyone indoors. To the right is protective fencing, designed to catch stray balls flying in from the ninth tee. The building has character and provides a tangible connection with the birth of the club, and if the walls could talk, there would be many a 'gawdy night' to relate.

It is the fate of many 9-hole clubhouses in the twenty-first century that they are seldom manned. The availability of a working coffee machine is as much as can be expected in many instances. If the Tee Shack were ever to be resurrected, it would be a welcome exception.

Leaving Covesea Links, the track climbs back to the B9040, and a left turn heads east towards Lossiemouth, skirting the RAF base and cutting through the Moray Golf Club. This comprises the old course designed by Old Tom Morris and the shorter new course, extended to eighteen holes by Sir Henry Cotton in 1979. Both are wonderful, I am sure, but it is a world away from humble Covesea. There is no sensible justification for Moray's fairways being so popular and Covesea's regularly empty.

Moray's imposing wood-panelled clubhouse is entirely in keeping with its chequered history. Such was the club's notoriety in the 1920s, that George Bernard Shaw was moved to visit Lossiemouth with the sole purpose of seeing *a place which has simultaneously produced the best prime minister of my time and the most stupendous collection of golf snobs known to history. Both should have a monument there.*[6]

On 1 September 1916 the Moray Golf Club members passed a resolution that Ramsay MacDonald's public utterances regarding the war *had led to resignations from the club and to a grave dissatisfaction among the members. The meeting also confirmed the finding of the council that Mr MacDonald's conduct was such as to endanger the character and interests of the club, declared that he had forfeited his right to remain a member and resolved that his name be removed from the roll.*[7] The motion was carried by seventy-two votes to twenty-four.

The national press was not sympathetic. An editorial in the *Aberdeen Press and Journal* on the following day observed that *it is not to be wondered at that the loyal members of the Moray Golf*

133

Club should desire that Mr Ramsay MacDonald's shadow should no longer darken the Lossiemouth golf course ... The Labour Party drove Mr MacDonald from its leadership when he talked his cosmopolitan twaddle at the outset of war.

Lord Elton's biography, published in 1939, confirms that *of all the incidents which took place in the campaign against him during the war years, that which, by common consent of his friends, he took most hardly was his expulsion from the Moray Golf Club.*

Writing in August 1915, MacDonald observed that *the golf club is infested by snobs and 'penny gentry'*, and later that year, *the Moray Golf Club has decided to become a political association with a golf course attached.*

And yet, for all the opprobrium targeted at MacDonald, his stance was not that of a pacifist, nor his views sinister. He believed Great Britain should have remained neutral, but having not done so, winning the war was imperative. It was his, apparently controversial, opinion that no opportunity for peace should be missed and that when it came, it must not be vindictive. The Treaty of Versailles was precisely that, making the next war if not inevitable, at least very probable.

George Bernard Shaw's judgement was possibly too harsh. The golf club's exclusion motion was not representative of the entire membership, and there were many, including the laird, who if not entirely supporting MacDonald's views, thought his politics irrelevant to playing golf on Stotfield Links. As John Ellwood accurately observes, ... *as has often been the way with golf clubs, a relatively small but determined group can get its own way.*[6]

Without a dissenting voice, the Moray Golf Club motion of 1 September 1916, which expelled MacDonald, was rescinded on 11 July 1929, but he declined the invitation to return, and on his subsequent visits to the area always played his golf at Spey Bay, where he was made an honorary member—one in the eye for the Moray Golf Club.

By the time of his death in 1937 his popularity was evident from the numbers awaiting the arrival of his casket at Lossiemouth Station and the nearly two thousand attendees at the Spynie Cemetery committal service on 27 November. *Deeply moving, homely incidents attended the last stage of Mr MacDonald's sad homecoming ... The end of one of the most sorrowful days in the history of the town ... in the gloaming of a winter's afternoon*—a distinct change of tone by the *Aberdeen Press and Journal* of 29 November 1937. His ashes lie beneath the family memorial stone at Spynie, together with his wife, daughters and sons.

Driving further east, the next destination is Cullen. The simplest route is to pick up the A941 in Lossiemouth and head south to Elgin, running almost parallel with the long-abandoned Morayshire Railway, the first line north of the Grampians. This short 5-mile railway was opened on 10 August 1852 to much fanfare and stayed in operation until 1966. Lossiemouth Station has been demolished, but the platforms are still in evidence in the park just south of the marina, on Pitgaveny Street, the head of the A941. *Among the local boys who watched the railway activities with fascination was James Ramsay MacDonald, who was born in a cottage a few feet from the line*[8]—1 Gregory Place, just 700 yards south of the station. The line also passed within a few hundred yards of Spynie Cemetery. A life beginning and ending in steam.

Once across the River Lossie at Elgin, the A941 joins the A96. Turning left and east, a succession of roundabouts eventually gives way to the open road and the 10-mile drive to Fochabers. The A96 bypasses the town and leads to Fochabers East Roundabout, where the A98 is first left, signposted *Fraserburgh*, arriving at Cullen after 12 miles. Arrival in the town is announced by a string of railway arches. A sharp left turn off the main road at the first arch is signposted *Beach, Golf Course*. The bay appears as if through a series of arched windows. Under the viaduct the road turns left, and the clubhouse is immediately visible, sandwiched between the railway embankment and the sea.

I have an emotional attachment to Cullen. I first came here in 1959, and initial impressions were not good. There was rain and steam in the air, while the eastern end of the bay was dominated by a gasometer, just like the one at home, adjacent to the Altrincham Council tip. It seemed industrial, and with the tact of an eight-year-old I said what others were probably thinking: "I don't like this much." Eventually, the sun came out and the reservations were forgotten.

> *Wait a minute, it's stopped raining,*
> *Guys are swimming, guys are sailing,*
> *Playing golf, gee that's bettah*
> *Muddah, Faddah, kindly disregard this letter.*
> (with apologies to Allan Sherman and Lou Busch)

A time of innocence, my first journey into Scotland was the best and most memorable of my early years.

I had just completed my third year at school. The world was a safe place and life uncomplicated. Other than an overwhelming desire to entertain, at home and in the classroom, I was not a difficult child. All of life's disappointments, embarrassments, high passions and betrayals—mine and others'—lay somewhere in a distant future, completely unimagined. I had yet to develop an interest in the railways, so the sight of steam engines trundling over Cullen Viaduct sadly passed me by. I was equally unaware of the golf course, despite its proximity to the beach—the place where I spent most of the holiday. I cannot have been a very observant eight-year-old, nor was I keen on instructions—*a capable worker who is making most satisfactory progress. If only he had read the instructions in his intelligence test with his usual care, his position in the exam would have been much higher* (end of term school report, 1959). *If only* ... It could be my epitaph.

My form mistress that year was Miss Kay, a woman always destined to be a 'Miss'. An unfortunate-looking lady, she had hair fashioned like a bird's nest, with a beak-like face to match. She was a shoo-in for Irma Prunesquallor.[9] Unlike Irma, Miss Kay—I never knew her first name—was a gentle and loving character whose care and attention to her brood of schoolboys possibly masked a deep void in her life. Her strange appearance was by no means unique. My world was peopled with a cast of eccentrics, peculiar forms of humanity which seem absent from the uniform world of the twenty-first century. I did my best to emulate them. My observational skills may have been lacking, but minor events I remember clearly. I remember mithering for a penknife emblazoned with a kilted Scot and bagpipes and immediately slicing my thumb—blood everywhere; I remember gurning in the holiday photographs, a different pose and face for every occasion; I remember a determination to go in the sea every day, regardless of the weather; and throughout everything, I remember my teenage sister as unconvincingly grown-up and immensely irritating. Most of all, I remember the stinging slap to the back of an unprotected leg—my mother, the executioner, never my dad. And there he stands, far right, not quite forty and sometimes mistaken for my sister's elder brother. I never imagined him gone.

Sixty years later I finally returned to Cullen, and my thoughts are no longer centred on penknives and the multifarious ways to irritate an irritating sister. I have progressed; I play golf.

Cullen Links is eighteen holes, but like many courses originating pre-1900, it started life on a much smaller scale. Established in 1870, it was extended to full length in June 1905 and opened to great occasion by Sheriff Reid from Banff. Extended by subscription for the princely sum of £60, the sheriff was invited to address the gathering crowd from the first tee. In among the grandiloquent delivery, ancient history emerges. Quoting from the Burgh Register of 1641, he found this reference: *James and George Duffus and George Stevinson convict by the Kirk session in break of the Sabbath for playing at the golff efteroone in time of*

*sermone and therefore are ordained everie ane of them to pay a
merk and mak their repentance the next Sabbath ... But while the
game of golf had been played there from 1641, it had not always
been played under such advantageous circumstances as it could be
that day. He believed the course at one time consisted of three
holes, which was eventually increased to six and afterwards to
nine holes, and now the players would have the privilege of
playing over this excellent course of eighteen holes (applause) ...
Mr Simpson, on behalf of the golf players, asked Sheriff Reid to
accept of a presentation iron club and to drive off the first ball.
Sheriff Reid accepted the club and, amid applause, made a capital
drive.*[10]

Standing at the first tee, while trying to summon a capital drive,
nothing quite prepares you for the joy of playing Cullen Links. It
may be the shortest of the eighty-four true links courses in
Scotland, but the lack of distance does not diminish the test, nor
the enjoyment. There are ten par 3s—some blind, some long, some
protected by rock and some a combination of all three. This is
crazy golf on the grand scale. And I loved it.

The first lulls you into complacency. An undemanding par 4,
Temple, gives no clue to the challenges ahead. But right there, at
the second, reality bites—not for the last time at Cullen, it's a
'where the hell do I go' hole. The answer is skyward, 40 feet up
and 111 yards along, in the direction of a rough, strewn bank and a
pin which might or might not be visible, depending on its position
on the green. Welcome to the real Cullen. This challenging par 3,
Farskane, is followed by two more: *Plateau* and *Den*. The long par
3, *Plateau*, runs parallel to the railway line—now an inland
footpath to Portnockie—so while the risk of pulling your drive into
an oncoming train is no more, the possibility of bagging a hiker

remains. The next par 3, *Den*, is short, but top the ball and you are in trouble; thick rough and a small ravine lie between the tee and the green.

Squeezed between the sea and the high ground above the bay, where the Great North of Scotland Railway once steamed, it soon becomes evident that the limited acreage available for golf demanded an imaginative course design. It was achieved by use of this high ground above Round Craig and Boar Craig. You can get some idea of the height achieved by standing at the foot of the town's railway viaduct as it towers above. Then consider this: by the time you reach the upper level of the course, the railway has disappeared into a cutting beneath the level of the fifth fairway, *Denside*.

As wisps of steam floated by carriage windows, railway passengers' first sight of Cullen would have been the sweep of the bay and plus-fours bedecked golfers playing the third. The engine would slow on its approach to Cullen Station as it crossed the viaducts and the full glory of Cullen Bay opened out before them. This journey was possible until 1968, when the line was closed with a swish of the Beeching axe. Fortunately, the viaducts were preserved and continue to provide a theatrical backdrop to the course and the fishing village of Seatown, Cullen. Even inland New Cullen, with its imposing Seafield Street, has a view to the sea framed by the most easterly of the three railway viaducts. Facing the sea, a road to the right of the main arch leads up to the site of the station. Demolished when the line closed, the route of the original line is buried beneath a housing estate. The possibility of restoration seems very remote.

The sixth, *Bay View*, another par 3, heads back east, parallel to the fifth fairway. The last of the holes on high ground, beware the rough crater to the left of the approach—wide right is better than tight left.

At the seventh, with one glorious drive into the unknown, you descend in a single blind shot to sea level. Forget the Pacific Highway; this is the best drive in the world. The joy of *Firth View* is the generous landing area. Clear the extensive rough in front of the tee, and you are almost certain to find your ball. And this highlights the delight of Cullen Links: for all its eccentricities, it is fair.

This image shows the view from the seventh tee, looking east towards the town.

The eighth, *Cruats*, is a short par 4 which takes you to the extreme west of the course, and the 194-yard par 3, *Sand Cheek*, completes the front nine as it heads seaward across the eighth and tenth fairways. This Old Tom Morris course takes you to extremities before heading back to the clubhouse.

If the main theme of the front nine is high ground, the theme for the back is hazards, some exceptionally large. The par 4 tenth, *Cup*, is a gentle opener, with only the burn to the front of the green to catch a short approach. Four successive par 3s now take you *Roon the Rocks*, as the members call it, a signature stretch starting with a 217-yard par 3 into the face of Boar Craig, the huge rock after which it is named. If you have kept your card together until now, *Roon the Rocks* is where it could all come undone. The eleventh green is small with undulating ground to the front, the rock to the rear and the out-of-bounds sea to the left. Be incredibly pleased with a par.

At the stroke index 2 twelfth, *Neaves*, it is not so much *Where the hell do I go?* as *Are they serious?* This image gives some clue to the challenge.

Playing over the eleventh green, the line to the 174-yard-distant green is the white marker post on the small hillock to the right of the eleventh pin. There is only one shot: straight and long. The challenging twelfth is followed by *Red Craig*, the rock now facing you to the left. It is another blind par 3 of just 127 yards, and once again protected by rocks left and right. If you are going to come up short, go left, as anything right will take a ricochet to who knows where. Clear the hazards at twelve and thirteen, and golf doesn't get any more satisfying.

Roon the Rocks is rounded off with a 202-yard par 3, *Blackfoot*, which skirts Red Craig to the left and ends at a green to the eastern side of Boar Craig. These consecutive par 3s are a delight and the defining characteristic of Cullen Links; if I could only play four golf holes for the rest of my days, I would choose these. It has much in common with holes six, seven and eight at Covesea.

The holes run out to the eighteenth, free of rocky hazards and steep climbs. The par 5 fifteenth, *Long*, tracks the Moray coastal path and beach to the left and finishes with a marker post atop a mound in front of the green. With the aid of a prevailing westerly, this could be a birdie opportunity, even for the moderate hacker like myself. The sixteenth, *Well*, a par 4, crosses the par 5 fairway, leaving just two par 4s, *Gushet* and *Home*, to play out to the clubhouse. *Gushet* is ranked as stroke index 18, but I am not sure why. There is trouble all the way down the right, and the green can be obscured by the second tee box and an elevated track. The solution is to add some distance to the hole and keep well left. After the challenges of the high ground and rocks, an undramatic eighteenth, *Home*, comes as a relief. The sea and railway embankment should be safely distant, leaving only a bunker to the left of the fairway as a final hazard. Sink your putt, sink a pint and sample the skink—the appropriate way to end a round at the nineteenth.

Cullen Skink in its most basic form comprises onion, potato, undyed smoked haddock and full-fat milk, but there is undoubtedly more to it than that. Indeed, it has now become an art form. The annual Cullen Skink World Championships are held at the Cullen Bay Hotel, where the best creators of this fine dish are pitted against each other in a blind tasting. In 2018 the prize went to Lynne Watson of the Lily's Kitchen Café on Seafield Street. Lynne is from Aberdeen. While Cullen is rightly proud of its local dish, the original skink was not even fish based. According to the *Dundee Courier* of June 1949, Cullen Skink is *a cottage recipe from the shores of the Moray Firth. Skink was usually made with leg of beef—this cheaper variety suiting parts where meat was scarce and fish to be had almost for the asking.*

In 1959 such delicacies were not part of the holiday experience, and as an eight-year-old, I would have been unlikely to have experimented with such exotic dishes. My mother would have dismissed such things as 'foreign muck' in her usual considered and objective manner. As I remember, the fare on offer at the Bay View Hotel was bland beyond compare. No wonder we consumed such quantities of HP sauce. Being sentimental, I would like to have stayed in one of the rooms again, overlooking the unchanged green at the bottom of Seafield Street, but sadly it is now a private residence.

On the clubhouse walls, above the Cullen Skink, there are small windows into a near-forgotten past. Despite the course skirting the beach, there are not many opportunities for even the wildest of hitters to reach the briny sea. Only at the ninth do you aim towards the bay, and it would be a monstrous misjudgement to reach the shore. However, that is not to say that there are no balls in the bay; indeed, there could be thousands.

On the original course map, at a position roughly in line with the current sixteenth tee, there is marked a battery, and on the wall of the clubhouse, an image of a row of cannons. The exact purpose of the battery is unclear, but presumably there was some thought to coastal defence. However, while possibly never fired in anger, they were certainly exercised regularly for Volunteers Big Gun Practice, a sport which bears some resemblance to foursomes golf. A press cutting from the time indicates that the match was halved:

On Friday last, this company, under the command of Capt. Ross and Lieut. Peterkin, fired off the remaining allowance of shot and shell for the year 1865. The day fixed on was anything but favourable for practice—the wind blowing a regular gale off the land—yet the detachments mustered at the stated time, nothing daunted, and it was a general remark of the onlookers at the battery that seldom, if ever, had such fine practice been made in like weather. ... The prizes [1,000 rounds of carbine cartridge] were to have been awarded to those showing the greatest proficiency in big-gun drill. The contest was judged by Adjutant Crabbe and in the presence of Captain Ross, ... when it was agreed that distinction or any individual superiority could not well be pronounced ... so that the prize came to be equally divided among the ten young recruits of the detachment, giving satisfaction to all.[11]

This begs the question, what did ten young recruits subsequently do with 1,000 rounds of carbine cartridge?

An image of the original small golf house, pre-dating extension to eighteen holes and the replacement clubhouse opened in 1908, is archetypal Edwardian. Men are behatted—mostly in straw boaters—ladies are demure and a group of bare-footed children loiter optimistically, one carrying a golf bag of equal stature. A pre-1914 image[12] of hope and innocence.

Another image shows none other than Ramsey MacDonald making an introductory speech at a Cullen golf competition at the end of July 1937. *The charm of golf was that the night before, one was fully persuaded that next morning one would improve. It did not matter whether one did or not. Where there was too much perfection and certainty, there was too much mechanism. If there were good golf in Elysian field, he thought Socrates would refuse to play with them if they used 10 irons.*[13] He was but a few months from finding out.

147

The prizes were presented by his daughter, Ishbel, who had been constantly at her father's side since the early death of his beloved wife, Margaret, in 1911. Elevated to 10 Downing Street's official hostess, aged just twenty, it was a role she would continue through MacDonald's three terms of office. Not until her father's death would she find the opportunity to marry.

Ishbel, like her father, was a keen golfer. Presenting prizes at a Banff golf tournament in 1932, she observed that *golf is the very best sport ... It is the only one I go in for, and I suppose that is why I think so, but one of the good points of golf is that you can play it all your life. I am going to play golf until I am seventy-nine, and then I can say I have played for seventy years.*[14]

Ishbel was married twice, her husbands dying just twelve and three years after taking their vows. She had no children and following the death of her second husband chose to live the rest of her days at the family home in Lossiemouth. She died on 20 June 1982, aged seventy-nine. Mission accomplished.

Notes

1. From Mervyn Peake's novel, *Gormenghast*. See Note 9 for the full quote and context.

2. This quote appears in Chapter 10 of George Houghton's *Golf on my Pillow*, 'The Uncensored Letters of a Midnight Golfer to His Son Across the Sea'. The precise source of the Sheridan quote is not supplied.

3. Andy Burnett quoted from *The Press and Journal*, 15 July 2014.

4. From Frederick Partridge's poem, 'My Ball and I are One', verse 1.

5. John Betjeman's, *Seaside Golf*, verse 3.

6. Extract from John Ellwood's article in *Golf Quarterly*, Issue 22, Winter 2016/17, 'How a Golf Club Expelled the Future Prime Minister'.

7. *Liverpool Daily Post*, Saturday, 2 September 1916, 'Mr. Ramsay MacDonald and Moray Golf Club'.

8. *Forgotten Railways—Scotland*, John Thomas, Chapter 11, 'Strathspey: The Morayshire Railway'.

9. A character from Mervyn Peake's novel, *Gormenghast*. The sister of Dr Alfred Prunesquallor, the castle's resident physician. *Vain as a child, thin as a stork's leg, and, in her black glasses, blind as an owl in daylight. She misses her footing on the social ladder at least three times a week ...*

10. The *Banffshire Herald* dated 24 June 1905.

11. With thanks to Cullen Past and Present and Cullen Links for unearthing the press cuttings relating to the battery.

12. This image, and that of Ramsey MacDonald, has been reproduced with the kind permission of Cullen Golf Club.

13. 'Cullen Ceremony: Mr R. MacDonald on the Game', *The Scotsman*, Saturday, 31 July 1937.

14. 'Miss Ishbel MacDonald on Golf', *St Andrews Citizen,* Saturday, 27 August 1932.

Heartlands

Chapter

10

Across the evening sky, all the birds are leaving.
Sandy Denny[1]

C ullen is the turning point. From here the journey south into the Scottish Heartlands must begin, following a route I can only guess my parents followed in 1959.

I remember much of the journey north from Altrincham to Cullen: a maiden trip along a UK motorway, the Preston Bypass, a near-empty stretch of dual-carriageway which was eventually subsumed into the M6[2]; the first sight of unfenced sheep as we climbed over foggy Shap; and the long journey to Callandar for an overnight stop, and the next day queueing for the Ballachulish Ferry, long before the bridge over Loch Leven was completed. I

151

look at the route we took and wonder what bizarre navigational plan my father was following.

The long wait at Ballachulish was not due to high volumes of traffic but the ferry's limited capacity—six cars in either direction. The lay-by for the ferry queue remains, such that sixty years later I was able to re-enact this moment in time, the family Ford Consul being replaced by my rotary-engined Mazda RX-8—not so much a car from a different age as from a different planet. At the time, I remember being very impressed by Ford's latest saloon, thinking it the height of modernity. My, how perceptions change.

The Mk II Ford Consul was 'powered' by a 1703cc 4-cylinder engine which developed 59bhp at 4400 revs, delivering a top speed of 75 mph and a glacial 0–60 mph time of 29 seconds. By modern day standards it was a dog, and closer, in terms of development and sophistication, to a Model T than any vehicle produced in the late twentieth century. The cars were poor, the roads narrow and the journey times prolonged.

The Ballachulish Hotel remains, but the horizon is now sullied by the utilitarian bridge which flies in line with the hotel's eastern turret. A few hundred yards west is the Dragon's Tooth golf course, something else that did not exist in 1959. Squeezed between mountain and loch, it is an interesting test of golf laid out on the slopes of Glenn a` Chadias and is another course constructed by Andy Burnett of Covesea. His company, Greenstaff Services, continues to carry out specialist annual spring and autumn course works.

By contrast, I remember nothing of the 1959 return journey from Cullen, other than it took forever. A heated parental debate in an unheated Ford Consul ensued throughout. In dispute: the wisdom of attempting the trip non-stop. My assumption is that we took a direct return route which led back to Aviemore and the A9 at a time when this main northern artery passed through every town and village. I am doing the same.

For the first time on this golfing pilgrimage it is necessary to retrace some steps, taking the A98 back to the Fochabers Bypass, briefly following the A96 west and then turning left, and south, on the B9015, joining the A941 just north of Rothes, home to four distilleries. Despite best endeavours, and sad to relate, I have never developed a taste for the water of life, and so there was no temptation to linger. At Craigellachie, the A941 becomes the A95 and follows the River Spey throughout its length, terminating at the junction with the A9, just north of Aviemore.

I had always planned to include a visit to Blair Atholl but could not decide where to play between this course and Cullen. And then I remembered a conversation with our greenkeeper and club secretary, Neil, that went something like "Have you not played Carrbridge? It is first class." The implication being that any itinerant golfer worth his salt could not possibly have passed it by. I confessed that I had not. In a satisfying example of numerical synchronicity, it transpires that clubhouse door to clubhouse door, give or take an inch or two, Carrbridge is exactly halfway between Cullen and Blair Atholl—56.3 miles from Cullen to Carrbridge and 56.2 miles from Carrbridge to Blair Atholl. This course was predestined to be included in *Golf in the Wild*.

It is one of those towns that the A9 has bypassed in its never-ending quest to take you nowhere. A few miles north of the A95 junction with the A9, the B9153 heads a short distance north to Carrbridge, where a few modest shops and a petrol station are followed by a bridge over the River Dulnain, with the imposing Carrbridge Hotel to the right. A keen golfer is sure to spy the not-too-distant, carefully tended green and the neat clubhouse, landmarks that might otherwise go unnoticed. A few hundred yards beyond the hotel is the entrance to the golf course.

I arrived on a bright sunlit afternoon, and it was immediately apparent that Neil was not wrong. The course is immaculately presented and in a perfect Highland setting. A neat, red-roofed, green-walled, twin-peaked clubhouse blends with the landscape—a clubhouse design which could date from the origins of the club. A round clock face, sited between the twin elevations, counts away the hours. Well-tended tubs of flowers sit astride the verandah, and a manicured path leads beyond the putting green to the first tee. Small things, but first impressions are important.

An advantage of 9-hole courses is that you know where you are in the world. Carrbridge has a discernible structure from the outset. Seven consecutive par 4s are rounded off by two par 3s. The first parallel fairways run east and west from the clubhouse. A north-facing drive across a valley at the fourth connects with two parallel par 4s across the top of the course, and the seventh returns over the same valley. Two pars 3s then wind their way back to the clubhouse. By contrast, there are immense 18-hole parkland courses in Northumberland whose geography remains a mystery, regardless of how many times I have walked their indist-inguishable fairways.

The first, *Lang Stracht*, runs parallel with the A938. The same illustrious Allendale golfer who planted a ball in the Portmahomack school playground tells me that a sliced drive can reach the coaches parked at the Carrbridge Hotel. "If the door had not been closed, I could have eliminated a few pensioners." The undulating fairway looks inviting, but it narrows at the distant red and white marker. A straight drive should clear the bank and come to rest on a lower level, at a distance from the burn that diagonally crosses the fairway some 280 yards from the tee. A 'big hitter' might find water, I guess, but this is not a problem for me—there are advantages to being an average hacker. A moderately good drive of 200 yards plus still leaves the same distance and more to the green. This is a challenging opening par 4 off the yellows but an easier par 5 off the whites.

A well-struck fairway wood is still likely to be short of the green; there is also a centrally placed bunker to avoid. As you cross the burn, a gong must be struck, J. Arthur Rank style, to advise those on the first tee that lunch is now served. My third, a pitching wedge, found the heart of the green followed by a satisfying two-putt. Avoiding a three-putt at the first is guaranteed to put me in a more positive frame of mind, and positivity is certainly required for the next.

At the second, *The Nest*, I clipped a drive an unusually long distance which, assisted by a down slope, ran too far left towards the first fairway and the burn. From down there, and probably elsewhere, what to do next had me perplexed. Protected by tall trees left and right and heavy, rough and minimal fairway, the green is nestled in a dip out of sight—hence the hole's name, I guess. I could spend a lifetime trying to master this hole. Every course should have one.

The third, *Lochanhully*, a more straightforward challenge, completes the opening section of the course, three parallel par 4s, after which a sharp left up a bank leads to the fourth tee and *Valley*. From the elevated tee, the downhill slope to a distant burn looks too easily drivable, and the longer the hit, the less of the elevated pin can be seen—a cunningly designed hole. The fifth, *Badengorm*, and sixth, *Cairngorm*, play in parallel across the top of the course. Set among carpets of purple, heather-lined fairways, it is a special place to be on a sunny September afternoon. At the fifth, tee and green are on similar levels, but the fairway slopes down to a drainage ditch at around 150 yards. A well-struck drive will clear this and then some before coming to rest on an uphill approach. A pitching wedge to within 4 feet, a single putt and a birdie at first attempt, followed by a par at the sixth, made for one happy golfer. Modern course designers, take note.

The seventh provides a similar optical challenge to the fourth—a distant elevated green with a near-vertical approach that looks drivable. I took a 7-iron and came up far too short. I took three to reach the dance floor and then three-putted from the back of the green. In a quick step, confidence can desert you. For over a hundred years this well-trodden turf must have seen many a round come to grief on and around the *Eyrie* bank. The eighth, *De'els Brew*, is the easier of the two par 3s from an elevated tee and would be very straightforward but for Park Cottage which sits just to the left of the final approach—clobbering the walls and roof seems all too easy. At one time it was owned by a former club president who would sympathise with the wayward golfer, but the current resident has no connection with the club and is not, by all accounts, keen on golf—an odd choice of home under the circumstances. There is some consideration being given to repositioning the tee to minimise close encounters. The committee has a streak of consideration which I do not share—buy a house in the middle of a golf course, and what do you expect?

The finale is *Hame*, a dog-leg par 3 from another elevated tee, which is approached by a steep, energy-sapping pathway. The reward for your struggles is a fine view of the Carrbridge Hotel and distant mountains. The green is around a corner to the right, near the clubhouse, and reaching it in regulation is way beyond this golfer's ability. At stroke index 2, playing into the sun adds another level of difficulty, especially for the lone golfer—*Where the hell did that go?* was my immediate post-drive reaction. Sad to relate, I never did find out. Another time I would accept my limitations from the outset, play it as a par 4 and hope to get lucky with my approach. It is a testing finish.

The Carrbridge Hotel architecture is Scottish Baronial and sits serenely in a wooded and mountainous landscape, an abiding memory to take away from the last. It is also entirely appropriate that this building should take centre stage, and not because itinerant Allendale golfers have a penchant for striking balls into its car park. The course came into existence entirely because the 1894 hotel proprietor, Peter Grant, was a keen golfer and saw an opportunity to attract more visitors to the town. Using land once occupied by the Old Market Stance, together with a stretch of ground each side, a 6-hole golf course was opened on Wednesday, 4 July 1894. There is a pattern to these events. The primary instigators continue to organise and work hard behind the scenes while the great and the good applaud and pay respects to the landed gentry who take centre stage. The speeches are the same—the health benefits for the local populace and visitors are extolled by a local dignitary who wishes good fortune for the club and its members while forecasting overly optimistic financial benefits for one and all.

On this occasion the honour fell to the colonel, whose over-corseted wife was given the privilege of driving the first ball. Unsuitably dressed and probably underqualified, according to the *Elgin Courant* of 6 July 1894, she *put the ball with the first blow*, although quite where and how far was not recorded. In the Hollywood film of this event, I would cast, in suitable period dress, Ballard Berkeley. He played Colonel Freddie Danby in the *The Archers* before being promoted to Major Gowen in *Fawlty Towers*. "Morning, Fawlty. Lovely day for a round of golf … Anyone here care to make up a four?" Not just an accomplished actor, Berkeley served as a special constable with the Metropolitan Police during the Second World War and was twice decorated.[3] I imagine a stern, forbidding character.

A fear of the police and authority was instilled from an early age, and it persists.

In the early 1950s the family home was still wired with pre-war round-pin plugs. Differently rated plugs were different sizes; a 5-amp plug was physically different to a 15-amp plug, and they required different sockets. The Electrolux ZA30 vacuum cleaner was fitted with a Bakelite 15-amp plug conforming to BS 546. Like many family homes, the house was not converted to square pin, BS 1363, until the early 1960s, even though the British Standard was first published in 1947.

There were some safety features associated with BS 1363, not least the shuttered socket which prevents a child pushing a nail into one of the holes and making a live connection. I remember no inclination to do so. The round pins were unsafe in other ways, not directly associated with BS 546: their Bakelite construction was prone to break, revealing deadly live wires.

One innocent summer's morning I was accused. "You have broken the vacuum cleaner plug, Robin! Half is missing. Where is it? You could have electrocuted me!" Mother was in full, exaggerated flow. "Where is it? Just tell me!" My denials went unheeded, and then, as if by magic, the broken part appeared on the staircase. More accusations; more threats. "Just admit it, or I am calling the police!" I was young enough to believe this a possibility. The imagined policeman arriving at the door was not a man in blue but plain clothes CID in a brown mac. Neither Sergeant Pluck nor Policeman MacCruiskeen, this third policeman was cobbled in my head from TV characters, none of them sympathetic. "Just admit it, and nothing more will be done." And so I did.

A stinging smack, and I was sent to bed for the day—no TV, and only toast for tea.

This was a valuable lesson. I learned that the truth will not always save you. I learned that under duress anyone can be persuaded to say anything. I learned that grown-ups were fallible, not always to be trusted.

I was completely innocent; so innocent, I never made the obvious accusation—my sister did it! Big sister kept quiet throughout, and who could blame her, given the onslaught I received? The magical appearance on the staircase was probably an attempt to pacify, except it only made things worse.

In the many days' pre-school, time eased along with the tortoise, whereas now it runs with the hare. This was the longest day. It was a pattern repeated and repeated down the years. Repeated until I learned that an imaginative distancing from the truth could be convenient; in a tight corner my imagination would run riot.

Hell goes round and round. In shape it is circular, and by nature it is interminable, repetitive and nearly unbearable. Flann O'Brien, *The Third Policeman.*

The course was laid out with advice and guidance from Mr Alexander MacHardy, chief constable, Inverness, described by Harry Ward[4] as Scotland's forgotten golf architect, responsible for laying out no fewer than ninety courses.

Conversion of Carrbridge to nine holes is undocumented. Newspaper reports in the summer of 1899 were still reporting tournaments played over six holes, *exciting contests as any played over many an 18-hole course.* Despite surviving two world wars and the added attraction of extension to nine holes, by the late

1970s the course had, over many years, fallen into a state of neglect. The 1978 leaseholders, the new owners of the Carrbridge Hotel, concluded that any benefits of a nearby golf course were outweighed by the maintenance overheads.

Carrbridge Golf Club may have disappeared altogether but for the enthusiasm and determination of local golfers. Members of a revived club first tried to meet at the village course in May 1980 but were confronted by two policemen who informed them they were trespassing, something that would surely never have happened in MacHardy's time. The lease disagreements were eventually resolved by Carrbridge Community Council, who negotiated the lease transfer back to the villagers. The club has since purchased the land, and its future is assured. The resurrection was a magnificent accomplishment, but some forty years later the presentation of the course is the greater achievement. Described by Council Chairman David Ritchie in 1980 as 'pretty wild', it is now pristine—perhaps one of the best-presented 9-hole courses in Scotland.

Driving left out of the club car park, I realise I will have passed this way on many an occasion in the 1970s, travelling down the old A9, homeward bound from the north-west. A non-golfer at the time, the course would have gone unnoticed, regardless of its state of play. I am but one of thousands who no longer pass this way since the A9 bypassed the village. No doubt welcomed by people living adjacent to the main road, local businesses may be less enchanted.

Regardless, the village still seems to thrive, to some extent assisted by its culinary connections.

It turns out that Carrbridge is to porridge what Cullen is to skink. Since 1996 it has played host to the World Porridge-Making Championships, where competitors from across the globe compete for the coveted Golden Spurtle trophy. A spurtle is a dowel-shaped spoon used exclusively for stirring porridge. Before the advent of rolled oats, constant stirring with the spurtle helped to eradicate lumps. A spurtle sounds like an agricultural implement that might have been familiar to Rambling Syd Rumpo, not something associated with food for human consumption. Nevertheless, the porridge-based concoctions that take home this annual prize are remarkable and only distantly related to the Scott's Porage Oats I was obliged to consume as a child. The misspelling of 'porage' was an intentional marketing gimmick intended to combine 'porridge' and 'potage' (a French word for a thick soup). The analogy is correct but hardly a mouth-watering prospect at the start of the day. By contrast, the 2020 winner, *Crunch Sa Bheul* (Gaelic for Crunch in the Mouth) by Chris Young sounds an altogether more salivating prospect.

Enough of wild oats. It is time to head a further 56 miles south. It is but a few miles to the A9, once the direct connection between a string of communities. Over the years, a series of road-widening and bypass schemes has meant you can travel vast distances without going anywhere. Transport Scotland have an answer to the resulting tedium: for its entire length, including the 60 mph stretches of single carriageway, lorries over 7.5 tons are slowed to a maximum of 50 mph, thereby creating any number of mobile chicanes on one of the most dangerous roads in the country. For further entertainment, the gantry signs convey illuminating messages: *Check Your Eyesight* (What? Now?); *Belt Up In The Back* (advice to mothers-in-law—Les Dawson would approve); *Check Your Tyre Pressure* (Which one?); *Be A Courteous Driver*

(Okay, I have been persuaded*); Do Not Be Distracted By Pointless Signs* (I made that up). Finally, as you travel at a snail's pace behind the largest articulated lorry outside Alaska, you can admire the speed and ease with which trains progress through the Highland landscape—the Inverness to Perth Line runs tauntingly close for much of its length. Consequently, the 50-mile journey between Aviemore and Blair Atholl simply flies by. This was not the case in 1959.

The sky-blue MK II Consul parked at Ballachulish (registration 331 ELG) had been acquired earlier the same year and no doubt still possessed that new car smell—a particularly pungent and possibly noxious aroma, much more so than the twenty-first-century equivalent. This had replaced the black MK I Consul (RMA 803), and the MK II would make way for the maroon MK III (431 LLG) a couple of years later—we were a Ford family. Without much foundation, I considered our MK II Consul much superior to any other cars in our short street.

Miss Bracher lived at the bottom of the road and owned a Wolseley 150. An ageing spinster, the Wolseley's long face was entirely in keeping with her narrow features and thin life. A few doors up, John's dad owned a Standard Vanguard. A slightly rotund young boy with a matching father, the American-inspired design, bench seats and column gear change were custom made for the oversized family. David, who lived next door, was a late baby; his bulbous Austin England was entirely in keeping with his too-old father and his bald pate. Cars were designed to match their owners, much like family dogs.

A parallel passion for the still image, I owe to my dad, who taught me the secrets of the dark room from a young age. I can still conjure him into existence with the smell of developer and fixer. He had no real interest in cars, other than new Fords, and even less in motor sport. When they became the centre of my teenage existence, we effectively went our separate ways and never found our way back. Given free choice, I would have joined the automotive industry but instead spent forty years only partially interested in computers—unreliable and unnecessary devices according to my dad. Taking up golf didn't impress him either, and, avidly anti-German like Major Gowen, he was even less impressed when I briefly acquired a BMW 3 Series; he referred to me as 'Joseph with His Coat of Many Colours'. It was metallic silver.

Long hypnotic periods at the wheel can result in an important turning missed. Helpfully, the B8079 for Blair Atholl is pinpointed by a shopping mall at its junction—an unlikely if convenient collection of shops selling a host of things you never knew you needed, made irresistible by their tartan wrapping.

Three miles along the B8079, the original route of the A9, is the small centre of Blair Atholl, with the elegant Blair Castle and extensive Atholl Estates to its north. Through the village, over the Bridge of Tilt, right immediately beyond the hotel, and the narrow approach road terminates with a bridge over the Perth to Inverness Line, the original Highland Railway, this section being completed in 1862. A green and white clubhouse lies beyond. The course sits as though in a vast amphitheatre. *On two sides it is bounded by the Rivers Tilt and Garry, on the right is the Tulloch range, while to the left are the Lude hills, and towards the south the entrances to the Pass of Killiecrankie and the heights of Ben Vrackie are to be seen.*[5] Blair Atholl has all the ingredients of a *Golf in the Wild* course and, when I played, was empty but for one other distant golfer. The course was effectively my own.

Established in 1896 and originally known as the Invertilt golf course, the formal opening did not occur until Friday, 2 July 1897. *For scenic beauty the course is exceptionally fine … it commands a splendid view of the surrounding romantic scenery. Prizes are to be competed for, and a good game is anticipated.*[6]

Squeezed into a much smaller acreage, the original course was considerably shorter, at just 1,850 yards, compared to the modern-day layout—2,739 yards off the yellows and 2,872 yards off the whites. When the course first opened, it quickly became apparent that the limited acreage had resulted in fairways with too many crossings and an overall length that was not considered an adequate test of golf. Within a short time an additional field had been acquired, and an extended course opened on 11 April 1903—at 2,414 yards, approaching the length of the modern-day version *with holes varying in length from 170 yards (the shortest) to 336 yards (the longest). Five of them are over 300 yards.*[7]

After a couple of perfunctory stretching exercises, I found the first a testing introduction. An elevated tee provides a striking view of Ben Vrackie, after which it is named. Groupings of trees lead the eye to a distant pin and green. Trees in leaf partly hide the only blot on the landscape, Shierglas Quarry, as by degrees it consumes Creag Odhar. The average club golfer fresh to the tee would do well to achieve a net par at this 433-yard, stroke index 3 par 4. I took six at this and the next two holes, *Baluan* at 339 yards (stroke index 15) and *Glen Tilt* at 308 yards (stroke index 9). Some days you must accept you are not on your game.

Baluan is, in practice, a straightforward, flat par 4 with only a few protecting bunkers to contend with. The third, *Glen Tilt*, another par 4, completes the trip around the central plantation and takes you back to the clubhouse, on an elevated green behind the first tee. It is a green shared with the ninth.

A short walk to the fourth, a tee set in the shadow of tall pines, this hole is a beauty. A 91-yard par 3, *The Bridge* is named after the railway bridge visible to the back of the green, which carries the Perth to Inverness Line over the River Tilt. A very handsome example of Victorian railway architecture, it comprises lattice girders and castellated masonry towers which *appear to have served no purpose other than to satisfy the Duke of Atholl.*[8] The scene is completed by a traditional semaphore railway signal to the front right of the castellated arch. The proximity of golf and railway is oddly satisfying.

A pitching wedge seemed the perfect club. I am not a long hitter, but from an elevated tee, and possibly wind assisted, my ball finished between the railway fence and green, while the pin was positioned at the front of the green—on the back nine I learned that a sand wedge was more than adequate.

From the top corner of the course, the fifth, *Tulach*, a 300-yard par 4, follows the path of the Tilt as it flows into the River Garry. If the route to the green is considered not too testing, the uninitiated may find the many undulations across the green a difficult proposition.

I duly three-putted. The sixth, a 194-yard par 3, continues parallel to the Garry, after which it is named. The proximity of these rivers has on occasion resulted in flooding of the course, but over time the depositing of sand and gravel has probably enhanced the playing surface, much as the river has done at Innerleithen.[9]

The seventh, *Shierglass*, at stroke index 1, is the toughest hole on the course and from the tee appears to be tight with water everywhere. There is a pond left and another to the front of the green. There is more room than is immediately apparent, and for those of a nervous disposition there is a temptation to play unnecessary lay-ups. Trees encroach the green to the right, and bunkers add to the excitement. Oddly, it all becomes so much easier on the back nine, as the stroke index is elevated by three.

The stream and pond delineate the boundary of the original course. The extension in 1903 seems to have been largely achieved by acquisition of more land to the north. The first tee was originally sited near the fifth, and the land occupied by the clubhouse was still outside the course boundary. Despite its limited size, the locals were rightly proud of their new course. The formal 1897 opening was celebrated with scratch and handicap competitions and an array of prizes, including a handsome breakfast cruet presented by the laird. This was followed by luncheon at the Tilt Hotel with much toasting, speechifying and praise for Mr M'Inroy, the Laird of Lude. The members were *altogether indebted to their large-hearted and public-spirited laird [loud applause] who had from the very first taken a deep interest in the club and met the convenience of the members in every possible way.* His son was appointed as captain.

To the great advantage of the club, golf was in the M'Inroy blood. On display during the luncheon was a trophy from the old

Glasgow Golf Club—a silver golf club with two dozen silver balls attached, each inscribed with winners' names. The first, dating back to 1787, belonged to the Glasgow club's first captain, Captain James Clark of the 83rd Regiment.

Played for until 1835, the 1824 winner was Mr M'Inroy's father, who was presented with it as a last surviving member of the original Glasgow club. The club also bears the names of Mr Lillie (1815) and Mr Duncan MacBean (1822), M'Inroy's respective father-in-law and grand uncle. *Though repeatedly asked to part with it to Glasgow Golf Club ... Mr M'Inroy has declined to do so, as he considers it a unique heirloom.*[5]

At the time of the Invertilt semi-jubilee in July 1921, the same trophy is again referred to in relation to M'Inroy golfing prowess, but it had been returned to the Glasgow club in the summer of 1913. Having been presented with evidence that his father had merely been a custodian of the Silver Club, he wrote, *I am satisfied that your club are the proper custodians of the Silver Club and will treasure it as an heirloom, as was my intention had it remained my property. I have therefore instructed my daughter to forward to your address the box containing the Club by passenger train tomorrow.*[10] There are now four such Silver Clubs at Glasgow Golf Club. *The three newest Silver Clubs cover the period from the resurrection of the club in 1870 and have a silver ball with the name and date of each captain since then. A new silver ball goes on each year.*[11] Sadly, a major fire at the clubhouse in 2018 resulted in the loss of some artefacts and memorabilia, with smoke and fire damage to the remainder. The Silver Clubs and their cases were damaged, but all have been successfully restored, including the 1787 Club.

William M'Inroy died in February 1916, aged 86. At the time of the semi-jubilee, his mantle had fallen to his daughters, and one Miss M'Inroy of Lude had been installed as president of the club. The semi-jubilee speeches acknowledged the club's debt to the laird and his family and described the Invertilt course as *the best 9-hole course in Perthshire, or indeed in Scotland, and while there was room for an 18-hole course, he counselled them to think well before going in for any larger scheme in preference to the 'top hole' nine holes.*[12]

Oddly, this sage advice makes no reference to the time when the course possessed the full eighteen. Intriguingly, there are several newspaper cuttings dating from 1911 which reference the extension. Opened on 29 July 1911, the course is described as *long at 6,028 yards and occupying some 93 acres, the longest hole being 520 yards and the shortest 110 yards.*[13] The additional ground was again granted by the Laird of Lude, William M'Inroy. An aerial view of the modern-day course shows a triangular area of land running north-west between the first fairway and the railway. This is almost certainly the site of the extended course, long ago returned to farmland.

The last two holes take you home, heading north-west towards the clubhouse. A short, stroke index 13 (16 on the back nine) par 4, *Bruar*, appears straightforward but has a sting in its tail. There is a pond protecting the green which is unseen from the tee. A good straight drive is not rewarded. Fortunately, on the day I played, the long days were shortening after a dry summer, and the pond was empty. A chip out of the hazard was rewarded with a par, but only by good fortune.

The last is the only par 5 on the course. *Creag Urrard*, at 508 yards, is a fine finishing hole with a blind approach shot to the elevated green in front of the clubhouse, which it shares with the third. Leaving the last, there is a fine drizzle, the amphitheatre hills are shrouded in mist and autumn is drifting in on a cold Highland breeze. This is how I know it's time to go.

Notes

1. From Sandy Denny's 'Who Knows Where the Time Goes?', written in 1967 and initially made famous by Judy Collins. Denny's classic recording appears on the 1968 Fairport Convention album, *Unhalfbricking*.

2. The Preston Bypass was opened in December 1958 by Prime Minister Harold Macmillan. The original 8.25-mile road ran from M6, Junction 29 (Bamber Bridge) and the M55, Junction 1 (Broughton).

3. Ballard Berkeley was one of the first on the scene at the Blitz bombing of the Café de Paris, London, 1941. *He saw the decapitated 'Snakehips' Johnson and elegantly dressed people still sitting at tables, seemingly almost in conversation but covered in dust and stone dead.* Rob Baker's *Beautiful Idiots and Brilliant Lunatics: A Sideways Look at Twentieth-Century London.*

4. *The Forgotten Greens: The Abandoned Golf Courses of Scotland* by Harry Ward, 'Carrbridge, Golf in the Highland Region'.

5. From a description in the *Dundee Courier* of Saturday, 3 July 1897.

6. Extract from the *Dundee Courier* of Wednesday, 30 June 1897.

7. As detailed in the *Dundee Courier* of Monday, 13 April 1903.

8. From 'Grace's Guide to British Industrial History', www.gracesguide.co.uk.

9. *Golf in the Wild*, Book One, Chapter 2, 'Selkirk & Innerleithen'. Last paragraph refers.

10. An extract from Nevin McGhee's 2003 book, *Killermont: The Home of Glasgow Golf Club*.

11. An explanation of the use of the four clubs from Nevin McGhee, who is also the archivist at the Glasgow Golf Club.

12. A. M. Meldrum of Pitlochry quoted in the *Perthshire Advertiser* of Wednesday, 13 July 1921.

13. From the *Dundee Courier*, Monday, 31 July 1911, and *The Scotsman*, 1 August 1911.

Chapter

11

The Borders...

While three chambers of my heart beat true and strong with love for another, the fourth, the fourth, is yours forever. Elbow[1]

urning right out of Invertilt Road, it is just over a mile before the B8079 returns to the A9, a few hundred yards south of Shierglas Quarry. Three further miles south, the Ballanluig/Aberfeldy junction takes the A827 west to that wonderful golf oddity, Strathtay.[2] This temptation must be ignored. The destination is south, following the A9 as it relentlessly goes nowhere, bypassing Pitlochry, Dunkeld, Birnam, Bankfoot and every village on the road to Perth, where it arcs south-west to south-east. The M90 is joined at the dismal Broxden Junction, a place where roads, cheap food and cheap hotels coagulate.

Seventy miles south of Blair Atholl, the M90 flies the Firth of Forth under the graceful spider's web that is the new Queensferry Crossing. When I set out on this golfing pilgrimage in 2012, construction of this alternative to the Forth Road Bridge was in its infancy; when we returned from Cullen in 1959 there were *no* bridges and *no* fast roads—all roads went somewhere. The hours cramped in the back seat of the Consul with my sister must have been interminable. I don't remember. To be honest, I struggle to remember how I kept occupied at any time. *I have nothing to do today but smile.*[3]

In my early teens I discovered motor racing, which filled my every waking thought, much to the detriment of my education. Prior to that it was playing in the street, irritating all family members and occasional trainspotting. The only other distraction was music, and this filled all the spaces. I think even my parents softened towards The Beatles, but as I migrated to Bob Dylan and beyond, the shutters came down.

The sheer volume of twenty-first-century music and supposed 'stars' is overwhelming. Back in the dark ages, the choice may have been limited, but it was consumed obsessively—each track of an album played over and over until every nuance, every lyric, was absorbed. If I had any opinions, they were about music. Albums were life's milestones—*With the Beatles*; *The Freewheelin' Bob Dylan*; *Blonde on Blonde*; *Bookends*; *Bridge Over Troubled Water*; *Songs from a Room*; *Unhalfbricking*; *Liege & Lief*; *Blue*; *The Dark Side of the Moon*.

I bought *Bridge Over Troubled Water* on the day it was released, 26 January 1970. I must have ducked out of college, caught the train to Oxford Road, Manchester, and walked down to Rare

Records, 26 John Dalton Street, the shop where Ian Curtis was employed in the early seventies—*the first step in his musical career*.[4]

Bridge Over Troubled Water is a fine album but not the defining work of art that is *Bookends*. Significantly, I had reservations about the title track. The first two verses work beautifully, but the third is over-produced, too dramatic and the voice of the narrator changes from gentle reassurance to brash optimism. It is not the same person. There is a reason: it is not the song Paul Simon intended. It was Roy Halee, the record producer, and Art Garfunkel who insisted on a third verse—the first two could be *runway material for a take-off that is waiting*.[5] Reluctantly, Simon wrote the additional material too quickly and in the studio, something he never usually did.

So, here is the thing: from the northern side, drive over the Queensferry Crossing when there is a high wind, keep to the 40 mph speed restriction and turn on *Bridge Over Troubled Water* at the first exit to the old bridge. Turn up the volume and listen intently as you cross the troubled waters. When you reach the first gantry sign on the South Queensferry side at three minutes four seconds, start fading the track out, and you will hear the song as Paul Simon originally intended—*a small hymn*,[6] a small masterpiece.

It was always my intention to find the most attractive route possible between golf courses, the drive behind the wheel being as important as the drive from the tee. However, there is no avoiding that *swathe of clutter stretching across the waistband of Britain*,[7] so the solution is to drive through it as quickly as possible. Modern road systems make this easy to achieve. The A90, the M90, the M8 and the A720 obligingly link up to swoop round the southern fringes of Edinburgh and join the A68 heading south. There are no distinguishing features along the way; all I ever notice is the long-established dry ski slope on the face of Caerketton Hill. This has been there for over forty years to *my* knowledge, maybe much longer. I always check to see if it is still in business, and sure enough, the grey unsnow-like slope remains. Journeys to and from Dundee in a series of unsuitable machines have etched this place in the memory. A dark blue Mini 850; a black Mk II Viva estate with Rostyle wheels and the long back window reminiscent of the Scimitar GTE; an Austin Healey Sprite MK II, complete with camping gear, wife and Irish Setter; a white MBG GT, the one with the overdrive switch on the dash; a 2CV which I drove north up the M6 with the roof down and wondered why progress was so slow—the back window worked like an oversized wind brake; and various Nissans. I could go on. Despite their primitive nature, none of these ageing machines let me down—something of a minor miracle.

Subject to volumes of traffic, it is a quick connection from the Forth to the A68 but "the road is so boring, my dear". These are the words of Win, who lived two doors up our street, and she is describing a first journey on the Preston Bypass. She was married to Fred, who drove a series of Aunty Rovers at speeds which I could exceed on a pushbike. The stately Rover 90 commanded the centre of the road as if in a funeral cortege; undertaking Fred was a regular occurrence. He died young.

Fred was a keen DIY man, in the mould of Barry Bucknell. I have a picture of him, measuring tape in hand as though sizing up a box. Fred and Winifred; it was like they were made for each other—an inevitable and intended union. Fred died in his sleep, so poor Win woke next to a dead man. Close to hysterics, she ran down the road to my mother, Peg, the first port of call in a crisis. Stoic Peg always knew what to do. She made tea, calmed the distraught Win and walked up the road to place pennies on his eyes.

The A68 unravels south, taking in Pathhead, Fala, the incline around Soutra Hill and the forest of wind farms at Dun Law powering a toaster or two. Descending towards Oxton, the road splits at the Carfraemill Roundabout, the A697 heading to Coldstream and the A68 continuing the 4 miles to Lauder. In the centre of Lauder, veer right to be on the western side of the town hall and its prominent clock tower. Just beyond the town hall, turn right at Mill Wynd, and Lauder golf course will be found in under a mile, the old clubhouse and generous car park resting on the side of Chester Hill.

Lauder seems a peaceful enough place, but it has a chequered history. The town hall was formerly the Tolbooth, built to collect tolls from market stallholders and used as a jail until 1843. In the seventeenth century those behind bars would include gypsies, tramps, thieves and witches. Witchcraft prosecutions in Scotland were three times higher than in England, as they became scapegoats for any number of small disasters: a cow that no longer gave milk; butter that turned bad in the churn; ale gone bad in the barrel; the laird suffering ill-luck at the nine-holes. Superstition had to blame somebody, and the belief in witchcraft held firm sway over the Presbyterian mind. Anyone denounced would be brought before the Kirk session, providing an inquisitorial task in which they reportedly took peculiar delight.

If in the judgment of ministers and elders the accused demonstrated even a hint of witchcraft, then the 'watchers' would examine her entire body for the Devil's mark. The 'jobster' would prick the witch to see if blood would come—the precise pass/fail criteria are not well defined. *Once condemned, the fate of the witch was sealed. She was conveyed over the hill to Lauder, securely warded in the Tolbooth there and speedily done to death by burning.*[8]

Across the road from the Tolbooth, the cruciform Lauder Old Parish Church acquired a watchhouse in 1830 as protection against bodysnatchers, who remained a constant threat until the passing of the 1832 Anatomy Act which legitimised the supply of cadavers for medical research. No wonder that Borders' myth, folklore and legend prevailed into the Victorian age and beyond.

The Lauder Golf Club was formed in 1896, initially based on land near the Stow Road and then moving to Chester Hill, where Willie Park Junior (1864–1925), golf Open champion 1887 and 1889, supervised the layout of the new course. As the course matured, and to celebrate his involvement, he was invited to give a demonstration match with his friend Iain Christie, and it was at this event, on 5 August 1905, that he set the professional course record of 70—out in 36, back in 34.

This grand event was enthusiastically covered by the *Berwickshire News & General Advertiser*, an extensive piece which included reference to second sight and psychic research. The Kirk Elders should have been informed:

> *It is a well-known fact, especially to such as are gifted with second sight and whose facilities are clarified by psychical research, that it is possible, under certain conditions, to hold communication with the shades of the departed. Quite recently, the shade of Thomas the Rhymer, which still haunts the Valley of the Leader, visited the Tower near Earlston and*

communicated prediction regarding Lauder and its golf course. The prediction was given in the Latin tongue, of which the following is a fair translation:

> *As sure as one and two make three,*
> *Lauder will deserted be*
> *By visitors,*
> *Unless some local interest be*
> *Aroused, and that right speedily*
> *In golf.*

There is no ambiguity about the Rhymer's predictions, such as was attendant upon those of the Delphic oracle, and therefore it is most desirable that the inhabitants of Lauder, with something like the sword of Damocles hanging over their heads, in the form of this prediction, should at once awaken their interests.[9]

A colourful piece, no doubt influenced by time too long spent in the beer tent. A little less alcohol, and the journalist may have reported the correct score—the *Berwickshire News* declaring a score of 71, out in 36, back in 35.

Sadly, the good people of Lauder did not heed the words of Thomas the Rhymer, a man so revered he was immortalised in song. Local interest in golf declined in the 1930s, to the extent that the town council elected to take over the running of the club in 1936. An inspection by professional greenkeepers indicated that if properly looked after and worked on continually, the course could be an asset to Lauder, especially if all the rocks were blasted or dug out, as they were wrecking the machinery. A permanent year-round greenkeeper was employed, but to no avail. By the outbreak of the Second World War, the club and course had ceased to exist. During the war years Castle Hill would play host to a Polish tank regiment under the overall command of General Stanislaw Maczek, who was charged with bringing the 1st Polish Armoured Division to battle readiness in time for the Normandy landings of 1944.

Polish troops and their tanks were a familiar sight across the Borders, and some remained even after VE Day. In a letter to *The Scotsman* in June 1945 from Captain A. R. McDougal, Lauder suggested that *although the war in Europe was over, the Poles had not finished 'making war'. They had tanks tearing along the roads in Berwickshire and tearing them up ... wasting petrol ... causing damage to farm property—crops, fences, gates and dykes.*[10] To this list, Captain McDougal might have added compacting of soil and damage to land drains on Chester Hill.

It would be sixteen years beyond the end of hostilities before the prospect of golf on Chester Hill was considered again. Resurrection came in the form of the town council and John Adam Scroggie, OBE, former deputy inspector general of police at Ambala Punjab, who donated £500 to the cause. A son of Lauder, John Scroggie would remember the course from its early days and presumably continued playing golf while stationed in India—the Kharga Golf Club at Ambala was established before Lauder, in 1891, it being among the oldest golf courses in the country. Retiring to Lauder, he would have been keen to play golf on the Hill as he had done as a young man. In addition to financial support, John also donated a trophy, the Scroggie Salver, which remains an annual club competition.

The clubhouse is adjacent to the top end of the sizeable car park. Despite the course closure and the arrival of a Polish tank regiment, this is the same building first opened on 20 July 1911 by Mrs Rankin of Allanbank. The original intention had been that Lady Lauderdale would be the guest of honour and declare the opening, but in a letter to the club secretary, one Mr Scroggie[11], she regretted her inability to attend *due to the damp day and my not feeling very well.* She continued in the manner of Violet Crawly, Dowager Countess of Grantham: *I much hope that the clubhouse will be a great comfort to the community at large, and that it will be the means of bringing many visitors to enjoy the beautiful air and restful quiet of our pretty town and neighbourhood. I may be ambitious, but I hope in time to see a flourishing hydropathic, for I am sure that Lauder is an ideal place for invalids. Wishing you all success this afternoon.*[12]

The description of the building in the *Berwickshire News &
General Advertiser* of 1911 suggests it is externally unchanged
since that damp opening day in 1911: *The pavilion, a handsome
erection, is quite an ornament to the course and will provide a
great boon to all who are likely to use it. It comprises two spacious
rooms* [under twin elevations] *... and there is a covered verandah
running the whole length of the building.* The pavilion has a good
view of the ninth/eighteenth and is but a short walk to the first
tee—ideal for this invalid.

Different tee positions vary the length of holes on the front and
back nines, but they are fundamentally the same. The first two par
4s start by climbing the hill. The first, at 359 yards, is lined by
maturing trees to the right and heathland rough to the left, but a
generous fairway should result in a safe first drive. Invisible from
the tee, and possibly from the lie of your second shot, a dip in the
fairway hides a pond to the left and a drainage ditch which
encroaches well into the fairway. An approach from the right is the
safest route, while anything too long should be held back by a bank
to the rear of the green. An overly ambitious approach will settle
among a group of lonesome pines. Although shorter, the second
feels a steeper climb but benefits from a lack of trees and pond,
although greenside bunkers await the unwary.

The third is a testing par 3 at 202 yards on the front nine and an
easier prospect on the back nine at 160 yards. It is a disconcerting
view from the tee, as the fairway suggests a green a long way right
of its actual location. Diagonal rough starting some 50 yards in
front of the green is likely to snag anything coming up short—into
the wind, a more than likely outcome off the front nine tee. I have
vague memories that this rough once included a drystone wall, for
this was once a regular haunt. Business meetings in Edinburgh

gave rise to drives up the A68, a hasty rush through the agenda and, with luck, time to call in at Lauder Golf Club on the return leg. Surreptitious rounds, sneaked in during company time, were the sweetest of forbidden fruit.

At this high point of the course, the views west are to Staunchley Hill, Lauder Common and Muircleugh, while in the valley, Lauder Burn weaves a path around Chester Hill, and the coast-to-coast Southern Upland Way heads south towards Melrose on its journey from Cockburnspath to Portpatrick. At the fourth the fairway heads downhill to a tricky dog-leg par 4—374 yards on the front and 409 yards on the back. Heading left, a copse of tall trees will block your approach. Long and right is the only shot which will enable a straight approach. Any second shot veering right is sure to be caught in the coffin-shaped bunker which runs about half the length of the green.

The fifth continues the downward trajectory with a funnel-shaped fairway which appears constricted from the tee. Heavy rough left and a line of trees right demand a straight drive, although the fairway does open out left after about 75 yards. A par 4 at just over 400 yards front and back, the rooftops and houses of Lauder come into view from the green and the adjacent tee for the sixth.

At 150 yards, the par 3 sixth appears undemanding, but I know from bitter experience that the hazard is unseen. Short of the green there is a deep, rock-lined gully with ball-swallowing rough and rocks that will rebound a golf ball to who knows where. It is a simple golf hole with the ability to wreak havoc on a scorecard. It should be an easy iron, but these things get between the ears of a long-playing golfer who has lost his edge. My game peaked coincident with an obsessive determination to acquire a Category

A motorcycle licence—no alcohol, early nights, concentrate, concentrate. The test was passed, and the trophies flowed. The two events were not disconnected. Since then it has been a slow decline; the confidence from tee and fairway has evaporated, but not so on the green—it was never there.

Survive that little tester at the sixth, and the seventh is at the opposite end of the scale. An uphill par 5, the ascent adds considerable yardage to a hole which is 482 yards from tee to green. The fairway only opens out after 100 yards, and then it is a long upward slog with no hazards until you reach a sizeable drainage ditch just shy of the green. In compensation there are no bunkers.

The downhill eighth comes as some relief, although punishing rough and drainage ditches add to the challenge, with one of them crossing the fairway 100 yards out from the green. These well-maintained water courses ensure that this heathland course remains playable throughout the year.

Finally, the ninth tee invites a glorious downhill drive over substantial rough before finding the wide fairway and an equally inviting approach shot over a dry ditch and a green adjacent to the neat clubhouse. If time and energy allow, the temptation must be to go around again. And therein lies the strength and weakness of all 9-hole courses—a good front nine, and there is a fear that this cannot be repeated on the same holes of the inward nine; a bad front nine, and the back nine holds the prospect of something worse.

From here the A68 continues south, tracking Leader Water to Earlston, where what little remains of Thomas the Rhymer's Tower is set back from the road, beyond the petrol station and an appropriately named restaurant. Also known as 'Thomas of Erceldoune' and 'True Thomas', the poet and prophet was born in Earlston around 1220.

I might have known nothing of Thomas. I might have had a life half-lived. But the summer of 1969 changed everything. First-love flew in on a firestorm—she took the pains of boyhood and turned them into feelgood.

In those formative hours and minutes, our lives entwined to the music of Dylan, Leonard Cohen and Fairport Convention. As the other-worldly voice of Sandy Denny filled the room where my friends and I spent many an afternoon, Saturn V rockets fired astronauts at the Sea of Tranquility and the Ocean of Storms. *What we Did on Our Holidays*, the raag-like *Nottamun Town*, *She Moves Through the Fair*, *Meet on the Ledge*—they were the soundtrack to a coming of age.

Two short weeks after we met, the Fairport's road manager fell asleep at the wheel of their van, hit the M1 central reservation just south of Scratchwood Services (now London Gateway) and finished upside down on the adjacent Mill Hill golf course. Martin Lamble, their drummer, and Jeannie Franklin, Richard Thompson's girlfriend, were killed, and the seeds of the group's fracture were sown.

At the time of the accident, recording of their latest album, *Unhalfbricking*, was complete. Released on 6 July 1969, *the group was determined never again to play the repertoire they had worked*

187

on so carefully and for so long with Martin.[13] We played it endlessly—the eleven-minute 'A Sailor's Life'; 'Genesis Hall'; 'Who Knows Where the Time Goes?'; 'Autopsy'; and the prophetic 'Percy's Song'. All of them seeped into our bones and helped shape what we became.

Throughout that same summer, a reformed Fairport Convention worked on another album that would continue in the direction set by 'A Sailor's Life', the track that marked the dawn of British folk rock, the reinvention of English traditional music:

> *Ashley Hutchings had spent weeks trawling through the Cecil Sharp House archives, consulting sages like A. L. Lloyd and assembling a set of ballads that would lend themselves to Fairport's approach. In August, after two months of rehearsal, we were in the studio, and by November Liege & Lief was out and selling better than any Fairport record before.*[14]

It was an album that told ancient stories and affirmed our idealised view of the world—*I'd rather a kiss from dead Matty's lips than you or your finery.* And yet, despite its success, Sandy Denny took against the group's travelling commitments and split to form Fotheringay. Ashley Hutchings, still traumatised by the M1 crash and harbouring a desire to delve further into traditional material, split to form Steeleye Span with Maddy Prior and Martin Carthy.

'Tam Lin', the penultimate track on *Liege and Lief*, and 'Thomas the Rhymer' from Steeleye Span's 1974 album *Now We Are Six* are intimately connected. Both are based in the Scottish Borders around Earlston and Melrose, and both tell the story of magical encounters with the Queen of the Faeries—Thomas the Rhymer's seven-year entrapment and Tam Lin's rescue. Colin Manlove, a Scottish fantasy expert, argues that they are *two halves of a whole—the first showing the beginning of the enchantment, the other the ending.*[15] Both were rescued from relative obscurity by Ashley Hutchings.

At the foot of the north-east slopes of the Eildon Hills, the Rhymer's Stone, erected by the Melrose Literary Society in 1929, marks the location of the fabled Eildon Tree where Thomas was bewitched into his seven-year entrapment. At the foot of the north-west slopes is Melrose Golf Club.

Those Saturn V rockets may have powered *Apollo 11* to the first moon landing in 1969, but it was not until the *Apollo 14* mission in February 1971 that NASA undertook real scientific endeavour. As his time on the lunar surface approached its end, Alan Shepard, astronaut and golfer, dropped some golf balls amid the moon dust, attached the head of a 6-iron to a soil sampler and proceeded to hit a series of unique golf shots. The first attempt took *more dirt than ball*, his second was little better but the third made sweet contact and, with no air resistance and a sixth of the Earth's gravity, it flew *miles and miles and miles.*

This singular sporting achievement would, many years later, inspire the entrepreneurial golfers of Earlston to a giant leap of the imagination. They once had their own course set on the high ground to the north of the village, but no more. Founded in 1906, it was laid out on Caldie's Hill near Huntslaw Farm, land owned by the Estate of Mellerstain. Like Lauder, the course was designed with the advice and guidance of Willie Park Junior, who visited the proposed site on 4 September 1906. He almost certainly travelled by train from Edinburgh to Fountainhall and caught the light railway connection to Lauder, where he would have received an enthusiastic reception prior to walking the chosen ground with Earlston's golfing elite. A relatively short 9-hole course at 2,095 yards, bogey 36, the elevated position, sandy soil, small quarry and a deep gully named *Howe o' the Hope* no doubt made for scenic and testing golf. The course was formally opened on 30 April 1907 to great fanfare.

Sadly, its first incarnation was relatively short, the course closing for the duration of the Great War and, in 1917, its fairways and greens turned by the plough in order to support the growing of crops for the war effort. Such was the damage, that it was not resurrected until 13 September 1924, when *Colonel Hope of Cowdenknowes performed the opening ceremony by driving off from the first tee.*[16]

Closure of the course during the Second World War was the final straw, and the course never reopened, despite several attempts in the 1990s. The land was sold by the estate in 2000, with any hope of golf returning to Caldie's Hill finally removed. Despite this, Earlston Golf Club continues and has a thriving membership, a series of fixtures at away courses throughout the year and against all odds, since 2000, its own course—on the moon. The ultimate *Golf in the Wild* destination.

The course was acquired from Moon Estates in November 2000—a rectangular plot, identified as Area F-4, Quadrant Charlie. The design took into consideration Shepard's groundbreaking experimentation, such that at 38,412 yards (approximately 22 miles), it is by some margin longer than any earthbound equivalent—buggies are recommended. The front nine is the longer of the two, comprising three par 5s, the longest being 3,192 yards off the whites. Such a course demands a unique set of rules. For example: Rule 1(d): Out-of-Bounds—*If a player launches a ball into orbit, it will be deemed out of bounds if it would take more than five minutes to find it*; Rule 8: Rabbit Scrapes—*If a player claims relief from a hole deemed by the player to have been made by a burrowing animal, the player will forfeit the game. We don't encourage the telling of tall tales at Earlston Golf Club's Moon Course.*

A golfing buddy of mine has played the course. He thought the layout superb, but the clubhouse lacked atmosphere. Once Richard Branson expands Virgin Galactic to include moon landings, I look forward to booking my flight and teeing up at Earlston's first, the very enticing, 978-yard par 3, *Drappy Watter*.

Meanwhile, back on Earth, the A68 continues south another couple of miles from Earlston before crossing the Tweed near Leaderfoot, the place where the River Leader joins the big river and its meandering route to Berwick and the North Sea. To the right of the road crossing stands the Leaderfoot (Drygrange) Viaduct. Standing 126 feet above the Tweed, its nineteen arches once carried the Berwickshire Railway on its northeasterly route from St Boswells to Reston. Nearly destroyed by flood in 1948, the viaduct never carried passenger services again. Repairs eventually enabled use by freight as far as Greenlaw, but this also ceased in July 1965. Following a period of neglect by British Rail, it was saved from demolition by Historic Environment Scotland, who took over responsibility for the structure in 1996 and assigned scheduled monument status.

A further half a mile south, and Melrose is signposted right along the A6091. From here until the right turn into the centre of the town, the road occupies the track bed of the Edinburgh to Carlisle railway, the Waverley Line. A land once dominated by steam and rolling stock leaves little trace of former glories, just an occasional parallel line of trees or unexplained embankments and cuttings—the remains of a fallen empire. At just over a mile from the roundabout, the B6374 leads down into the town centre and emerges through a constricted road width to the market square and its Mercat Cross. An immediate sharp turn left up Dingleton Road leads under the A6091 flyover, once a railway bridge adjacent to the Melrose Station. Melrose Golf Clubhouse is to be found less than half a mile up the hill, set back from the road on the left. The road continues climbing, as do the parallel fairways—you immediately get some idea of what is in store.

From the lowest to the highest points on the course, the first to the fifth tee, it is a climb in excess of 210 feet. However, such is the stop-go nature of golf, that even the most ancient of limbs will find the ascent of no great significance. Add in a few minutes' rest and diversion looking for balls in the rough, and it becomes a walk in the park.

The club was formally established on 3 April 1880, although there is newspaper evidence of play across the base of the Eildons as early as 1874. It is a 9-hole course that has remained remarkably like its original construction throughout its history. As early as 1912 there was correspondence with the *Southern Reporter* extolling the virtues and local support for extension to eighteen holes:

Many influential gentlemen in the neighbourhood are greatly enamoured with the proposal, and I believe the majority of the Civic Fathers are also in favour of it. Colonel M'Neile of Kippilaw very generously offered the Bowden Moor field ... But I imagine the extension could be carried on the ground already occupied by the club ... Of course, a bazaar would be necessary to raise funds ... but the ladies would certainly not be found wanting in such a cause. H. S. B. Melrose, 4 November 1912.

Despite the influential support, the course extension never happened, and the services of the ladies were never invoked. It is perhaps for the good; as anyone involved in running a golf course appreciates, the cost of operating an 18-hole course is significantly greater than twice that of a 9-hole. As the clubs in the twenty-first century struggle to attract members, especially the young, it is perhaps the 9-hole courses that stand a better chance of long-term survival.

A diagram of the 1907 fairways depicts the same route and orientation as the modern-day layout. Indeed, the original hole names are retained at all but the first and second. Teeing off from the yellows, the opener, a 251-yard par 4, *Safety First*, starts the ascent and appears a gentle introduction, although any uphill fairway is going to add distance; the left to right slope of the fairway will punish the merest hint of a slice with a trip to the rough. Add to the mix a fairway bunker, three greenside pot bunkers and a horseshoe ditch to the rear, and there is plenty to trip the unwary. Originally just 170 yards and known as *Doctors*, in Germany it would have been called *White Gods*, not so much out of reverence as irritation at their inflated social standing. The medical reference at the first may have related to Melrose Asylum, sited directly across the road. Originally known as the Roxburgh, Berwick and Selkirk District Asylum, it opened in May 1872, was extended in 1899 and became part of the NHS in 1948, when the name changed to Dingleton Hospital. The site finally closed in 2001, the main hospital building being converted to apartments, and new housing occupying the grounds.

In 1883, the five-year-old son of the asylum's chief attendant sneaked onto the course, and so began a young boy's passion for the game of golf. In 1899 William Wilson became the professional at the nearby Selkirk club and then emigrated to the US, where he would take up professional posts at Pinehurst and the York Country Club, Maine. At the end of his career he estimated that he had given over 100,000 golf lessons. Among his students were the Russian and Japanese delegates to Theodore Roosevelt's 1905 Peace Conference and Mark Twain. This latter convert supports the proposition that *golf is a good walk spoiled* is incorrectly attributed to Twain. William died in 1959, aged ninety. The course at York Country Club was renamed the William Wilson Course in memory of its long-serving professional.

The second, *The Brae*, a 345-yard par 4, continues the climb towards the top of the course, following the line of Dingleton Road as it heads south around the western side of the Eildon Wester Hill. Having negotiated the testing slopes of the second green, it is a short walk right to the third tee and the prelude to three characterful holes—Melrose's answer to Amen Corner. The par 3 third, *Milestone*, is ranked the easiest hole on the course, but it is still a test.

In spring, bright yellow gorse lines the twin banks that line the approach—very pretty to look at, but a devil if you stray into its clutches. Over-clubbing and going long is perhaps the safest tactic for those of a nervous disposition.

Next comes the fourth, a par 4 dog-leg, *Klondyke*, which skirts the third green and heads left at about 200 yards, before a steep ascent to a generous green. A par here makes you feel like a proper golfer; a bogey 5 has much the same effect.

The key is positioning from the tee. Too far left, and your approach is blocked out, and too far right will find the rough. Unique on the course, there are no bunkers. Rightly so; this is challenging enough without sand traps.

To complete this classic turn for home, the fifth, a short par 4, *Butts*, provides the glories of an elevated drive, some 30 feet above the green. Short it may be and the drive enticing, with magnificent views of the Eildon Hills beyond the green, but all sorts of troubles await. Out-of-bounds runs the length of the hole to the right, a burn meanders the borders of the fairway to the left, feeding a pond within driving distance, and the same burn fronts the bunkered green. To the rear of the putting surface there is uncomfortably close, heavy gorse. Survive the turn with your card intact, and a green tartan jacket is within grasp. It can surely look no worse than the Augusta equivalent.

The glory of Melrose is its maturity—beautifully wooded, with clear definition to every fairway and approach. This is one of the joys of playing across land which has been trampled by golfers' soles for well over a hundred years. When Jay Griffiths wrote, *On a golf course nature is neutered ... Golf turns outdoors into indoors ... the grass is not singing. The wind cannot blow through it. Dumb of expression, greenery made stupid, it hums a bland monotone in the key of the mono-minded,*[17] she can surely have never experienced the joys of golf in wild places.

The Melrose course in the lee of the hills which define it, and the nearby town, significantly enhances rather than detracts from the landscape. People have been drawn to this place since the dawn of time. Atop the twin peaks of the Eildon Hills there was a prehistoric fort and Roman signal station. When, in 1950, the golf club successfully applied to the town council for permission to play on Sunday, the Sabbath was not the provost's key consideration; it was that golf might interfere with the rights of the people using any of the fourteen rights-of-way across Dingleton Common to the Eildons.[18] Never has there been any suggestion that the course in some way diminishes this ancient landscape.

The modern-day OS map is mostly devoid of footpaths on or near the course, St Cuthbert's Way passing at some distance as it tracks east to Lindisfarne. Consequently, the next three par 4 holes, *High*, *Pandy* and *Marks* can be played without fear of public intrusion. It is the slopes and fellow golfers that might present the risk, all three drives from the tee offering limited vision of what lies beyond. The descent is gentle, and the three fairways are blessed with magnificent views as you head for home, a major part of the descent being saved for the last.

There is a memorable structure to Melrose: the steady climb up the first and second, the glorious turn at the summit, the three isolated par 4s along the back of the course and then this, the final soaring drive down the last, *Home*. (*Home*, the original name for the hole, is sensibly assigned to the eighteenth—the ninth is *Ca' Canny*.) A short par 4 at 270 yards, it is a daunting drive. The fairway is narrow, with trees and rough to the left, but it is stray shots to the right that worry.

A burn runs down the right, and beyond is a tarmac drive leading up from the clubhouse. There is the distinct concern that a sliced drive could hit the hard stuff and bounce the ball towards the clubhouse, the car park and beyond. Successfully negotiate the drive, and the approach is protected by the same burn crossing in front of the green and feeding a pond to the left. A small green is further protected by two bunkers. Finally, anything long will run off the back of the green and down a 4-foot drop. It is a testing but very memorable finish.

I have played the course on many occasions, as it is an easy day trip from my home town of Hexham. When my youngest was the same size as my carry bag, we spent many happy rounds beneath the Eildon Hills. Now he towers over me like Dustin Johnson. Much has changed in the intervening years, but Melrose remains as glorious as ever.

Notes

1. Guy Garvey's lyrics from the Elbow track 'This Blue World', the first track on their 2014 album, *The Take Off and Landing of Everything*.

2. See Chapter 3, *Golf in the Wild*, 'Bishopshire and Strathtay'.

3. Lyrics from 'The Only Living Boy in New York', my favourite track from Simon & Garfunkel's *Bridge over Troubled Water*.

4. A quote from Joy Division Central—www.joydivisioncentral.com. Curtis was Joy Division's lead singer from the time of their formation until his suicide in May 1980, aged 23.

5. Art Garfunkel quoted from the documentary, *The Story of Bridge Over Troubled Water*.

6. Paul Simon quoted from the same documentary as Note 5.

7. *Golf in the Wild*, 'Journey 2: To Fife'.

8. *Berwick Advertiser*, Friday, 2 July 1915. An article entitled 'Witch Burning at Lauder'.

9. *Berwickshire News & General Advertiser*, Tuesday, 22 August 1905, 'Golf: Lauder Course—Exhibition of the Game', Willie Park Junior, ex-champion.

10. *The Scotsman,* Friday, 15 June 1945, 'Damage by Polish Tanks'.

11. Competition reports from this time list three Scroggies: H.F, J.A and J.H.

12. *Berwickshire News & General Advertiser*, Tuesday, 25 July 1911, 'Lauder Golf Pavilion'.

13. End paragraph, Chapter 20, Joe Boyd's *White Bicycles*.

14. Chapter 28, Joe Boyd's *White Bicycles*.

15. Farrell, M. (2009). *The Ballads of Tam Lin and Thomas the Rhymer: Transformations and Transcriptions.* Glasgow University.

16. *The Scotsman*, Tuesday, 16 September, 1924.

17. *Wild: An Elemental Journey*, Jay Griffiths, Part 1, 'Wild Earth: Absolute Truancy'. This polemic appears on page 6 of a 420-page tome, suggesting the author was keen to get this off her chest quickly. It points to an early life, traumatic experience with a golf ball.

18. Golf section of the *Berwickshire News and General Advertiser*, 25 April 1950.

Going Home

Chapter

12

It's not far, just close by
Through an open door
I am going home.
William Arms Fisher[1]

The walk down Dingleton Road to Melrose Station is a
welcome half-mile stroll after the ups and downs of the
golf course. Golfers with carry bags heading for the late
afternoon train must have been a regular sight for many years. Just
beyond the A6091 flyover there is a left turn into Palma Place, and
at the top of the short incline is the well-preserved station building.
Completed in 1849 in the Jacobean style, the *Border Advertiser*
described it as *the handsomest provincial station in Scotland*.
Many of the stations on the Waverley Line were demolished

following closure in 1969, so the Melrose building was fortunate to survive.

Assigned Category A listing by the secretary of state in 1981, the fully restored building was reopened for small business use by Malcolm Rifkind in 1986. However, the real surprise is to be found at the end of Palma Place. In the left-hand corner of the car park, a footpath rises some 40 yards and emerges onto the fully preserved up-platform, complete with its full-length, original iron and timber canopy. As traffic on the A6091 hurtles by a few feet beyond, it is a permanent reminder of Beeching's folly. Closure of the Waverly Line was probably the most contentious and short-sighted of them all.

Closed in January 1969, there have been reinstatement campaigns ever since. The most significant testament to this destructive transport policy was the reopening of the line from Edinburgh to Tweedbank in September 2015. Known as the Borders Line, even this initiative is under-invested, almost half-hearted. Built as a single track, with limited passing loops and unelectrified, it is dogged by the same limitations as the Far North Line: a restricted timetable, unreliable rolling stock and disruption across the entire service when out-of-service diesel units need to be recovered. A line that was limited in scope by 'experts' who forecast low passenger numbers was, by 2018, being forced to address overcrowding issues. In 2019, passenger numbers exceeded two million. This lack of vision is also exemplified by the termination of the line at Tweedbank instead of going the extra 1.5 miles to Melrose, a primary centre for the Borders' tourism, with a ready-made station and platform. The campaign to reopen this line all the way to Carlisle seems almost secondary to addressing the issues related to the existing infrastructure.

●

I am going to take an imaginary journey. For the last part of this pilgrimage, I will park up the car in Palma Place and join the ghosts of golfers who regularly took the train from Melrose to Newcastleton. After a round of golf at Newcastleton, I will catch the train to Hexham, via Riccarton Junction, and then join a connecting service to Allendale. It is a short walk from the station to Allendale's old course at Thornley Gate, where the journey will end.[2]

An afternoon Edinburgh to Carlisle service arriving into Melrose would regularly be pulled by a Gresley Class A3, 60093, *Coronach*, out of shed 12C, Port Carlisle. This 4-6-2 locomotive, introduced in 1927, worked the Waverley Line for much of its existence. Leaving Melrose, the line headed briefly east before arcing south towards St Boswells, just six minutes down the track, and the only scheduled stop before Hawick. On the approach to St Boswells the line used to cut through the centre of the Monksford Estate, which in the twenty-first century is home to a private 9-hole golf course, maintained for the exclusive use of the owner's family. After a brief stop at St Boswells, the A3 would steam through Charlesfield Halt, Belses and Hassendean before arriving into Hawick twenty-four minutes after leaving Melrose, assuming the service was running to time.

When the line closed, Hawick acquired the unenviable distinction of being the furthest major settlement from the UK rail network. The Border towns had fought long and hard to save their railway, but to no avail. The last train of all was the 21:55 Night Midland from Edinburgh to St Pancras. *The people of Hawick, who so often heard the Night Midland and its predecessors climbing away into the Border hills, heard the familiar sound for the last time ... A lone piper played that most soulful of Scottish laments, the 'Flowers of the Forest', a dirge heard traditionally at the end of lost battles and at the funerals of the great.*[3] A coffin addressed to the minister of transport, Richard Marsh, was lowered into the guard's van.

Leaving Hawick, at the end of the down-platform, a crowd of becapped, trainspotting schoolboys would be unexcited by this too-familiar A3. Heading south, the line begins its long slow ascent into bleak, empty moorland. The train would ease into Stobs, a station located in the middle of nowhere, the only significant place of residence being the nearby Stobs Castle. This was not always a place of solitude. In 1903 a military training camp was established on the Stobs Estate, and throughout the Great War it variously housed military personnel, internees and prisoners of war. As a result of an inspection in 1916 by a representative of the US Embassy, we have a precise analysis of the 4,616 prisoners detained at that time: 1,829 were soldiers, 504 were sailors and 2,283 were civilians. Of the civilians, 2,098 were Germans, 181 were Austrians, 3 were Turks and 1 was Bulgarian.[4] A sizeable garrison for nowhere land.

The volume of passenger traffic was so overwhelming that the camp established its own station on a short branch line at Acreknowe, half a mile to the north. Activity at the camp subsided between the wars but expanded again from 1939. The precise nature of military activity during the Second World War has never been revealed. Set on the exposed hills above Stobs Station, the wet, grim and permanently windy camp was unpopular with soldiers and prisoners alike.

> *Too true—it is a rotten hole,*
> *A dreary, cheerless place.*
> *And to Bonnie, Bonnie Scotland,*
> *A damnable disgrace.*
> *But if I swore from morn till night,*
> *The half I'd never tell,*
> *And so, I think I'll save my breath*
> *And simply call it hell.* [5]

The camp was finally closed in 1959, and all evidence of its occupation erased. However, look at any aerial view of the old estate, and the delineation of camp roads and huts remains clearly visible.

The climb towards the summit would have been no less bleak, the line from Hawick following Slitrig Water to its source. At Shankend, the magnificent fifteen stone-arched viaduct flies Langside Valley, which sits between Burnt Craig and Shankend Hill. The imposing white Shankend farmhouse would have been clearly visible from the left-hand train windows as the A3 rolled into the station, just over 100 yards south of the viaduct. Also on the left was the substantial station building, and beyond that, the signal box which controlled the adjacent goods yard. There is little else for miles.

From Shankend it was just a 4-mile incline to the 1,208-yard-long Whitrope Tunnel and the 1,006-foot summit 300 yards beyond. Started in September 1859, construction was problematic from the outset. Excavations started from the two portals, with five access shafts at regular intervals along the S-shaped route. Built beneath a lochan fed by several streams, upwards of 600 navvies worked in appalling conditions, the horse-drawn pumps unable to cope with the huge volume of water constantly pouring into the tunnel workings. Conditions were only partially improved by the introduction of steam-driven pumps. Almost a year behind schedule and significantly over budget, the first train passed through the tunnel on 1 July 1862, and the route of the Border Union Railway opened throughout its 98-mile length from Edinburgh to Carlisle.

The name Waverley first appears in railway documentation from the end of 1862, and from then on the company did everything it could to associate the line with Sir Walter Scott and his novels. The first engines designed specifically for this route, the 1876 Drummond 4-4-0, included a locomotive called *Abbotsford*, the name of Scott's house near Melrose.

After the summit it was an easy passage for the A3 as it descended an average 1:75 gradient, passing through Riccarton Junction and Steele Road and arriving into Newcastleton (also known as Copshaw Holm) not much over an hour after leaving Melrose. Leaving the train, the exit to the course was over a lattice footbridge by the level crossing and signal box. It was then a short walk up the hill to the golf course.

The history of the course dates from 1894. It was formed by two prominent villagers: Mr Alex Thompson, manager of the Newcastleton branch of the British Linen Bank, and the Rev. William Vassie, minister of the Castleton Parish Church. The membership comprised forty-seven men and ten ladies from a local population of just 1,000.[6] Described as a 9-hole course, it was seven, the first and fourth greens being played twice from the ninth and eighth tees respectively. While the original course shares some of the ground used by the current layout, a major difference is the siting of the first tee. In 1894 it was no more than a couple of hundred yards from the station, a short walk to some steps at the first bend in the road, which led up through trees to the start of the course.

Consequently, the first would have played across the Newcastleton to Langholm road, uphill to what is now the ninth green, parallel with the modern-day approach road. It was quite some opener—a par 4 climbing 124 feet in just 256 yards (a 1:6.2 gradient). My only experience of a similarly steep opener is the first at Colvend on the Solway Coast, in Dumfries and Galloway—it climbs just under 100 feet in 251 yards (a 1:7.5 gradient) and demands use of a portable oxygen concentrator. Motorised access to the first seems the better option. There is a belief that this first tee was eventually moved across the road to a position just above the John Byers Monument. Perhaps there had been just one too many close encounters with motorised and horse-drawn traffic traversing the Langholm Road.

John Byers (1879–1968), known as 'Bluebell', was the 'Bard of Liddlesdale'. A writer of poetry and prose, he had a deep affection for the surrounding moorland and hills. He had an intimate knowledge of the valley's history, which he articulated in his most successful book, *Liddesdale, Historical and Descriptive*, published in 1952. Writing in the *Southern Reporter* in 1942, he observes that *the moorlands attract us as the north attracts the needle of the compass ... Before pestering your doctor with your common, everyday complaints, try what the hills will do for you.* He was obviously not familiar with the first at Newcastleton.

Although formed in 1894, golf on Holm Hill has a chequered, on-off history. Local support has usually been strong, but what got in the way? "Events, dear boy. Events," as Harold MacMillan allegedly once said. Newcastleton is a sleepy place, only occasionally disturbed by the sound of raucous motorcycles seeking empty, twisting tarmac to the north. With the closure of the railway, the place became sleepier still. Nevertheless, the town was not immune to the tide of history.

World conflicts around the turn of the nineteenth century had a major impact on leisure activities in general and golf in particular. Closing around 1904, the course did not open again until 1920. Membership remained at sustainable levels up to 1924/25 but there was a sudden decline in 1926, followed by another closure, probably because of the General Strike, followed by the depression. Reopening in 1934, membership surged, and the course prospered until 1939. Closing for the duration of the Second World War, it would not reopen again until 1974.

On this occasion world events had a positive impact. The final and most successful resurrection was made possible by a small group of travelling golfers known as the 'Copshaw Bandits', who played regularly at Powfoot, some 30 miles from Newcastleton. On 6 October 1973 Egyptian and Syrian forces crossed ceasefire lines to enter the Sinai Peninsula and the Golan Heights, territory held by Israel since the 1967 Six Day War. By 25 October the coalition of Arab states had been humiliated. In retaliation, the Organisation of Arab Petroleum Exporting Countries (OPEC) proclaimed an oil embargo, targeting nations perceived as supporting Israel. Petrol prices went through the roof and supplies dried up, with long queues and fights breaking out at UK petrol stations. The Copshaw Bandits would have to look closer to home for their golf, and so the seeds of the resurrection were sown.

In the intervening years, cows, moles and sheep had free access across Holm Hill. The old fairways were covered in waist-high bracken and hawthorn trees. Bringing the course back to a playable state would be a mammoth task. Someone with an eye to history sought permission from Roxburgh Council to site the first tee in its original position across the Newcastleton to Langholm road. It turned out that the county planning officer, George Ovens, was an accomplished golfer who later became president of the Scottish Golf Union. He, in turn, recommended the design services of John Shade, a professional from Duddingston Golf Club, Edinburgh. Shade inspected the course on several occasions, and his final proposal included six new fairways and greens, with only the third and ninth greens being used from the original layout—an ambitious plan for a club with no money. Sadly, the plan to resurrect the original first fairway was abandoned.

The layout of the course, as perceived in 1974, is much as it is today. Perhaps the most significant improvement is that from 1979 the entire course was fenced and Newcastleton golfers were no longer required to dodge cowpats and negotiate fenced greens and tees. The wayward golfer would no longer be cowed by the unpreferred lie.

The steep ascent from the Langholm Road tee may be gone, but there is still climbing to be done. First impressions can be deceptive. The approach road is rough in parts, and the clubhouse has seen better days. The walk to the first is slightly unkempt, and the view up the first fairway a blank canvas—the green is out of sight, and, but for the length of grass, nothing much hints at golf. Do not be deterred; this is as good as golf in the wild gets.

The par 4 first, *Charlie's*, the par 3 second, *Wee Hill*, and the par 4 third, *Holm Hill* combine to climb to the top of the course, a change in elevation of some 180 feet. Much of the ascent is achieved at *Wee Hill*, a testing uphill shot to the green. Relatively straightforward at 106 yards on the front nine, but a more difficult prospect at 144 yards on the inward nine. A narrow path leads from the back of the second green to the third tee, another blind uphill drive with heavy rough to the front and right but with plenty of space to the left. The legs may be struggling at this point, but the climb is worth every step. The views are stunning and unchanged since the 1894 *Evening Dispatch* reporter dragged himself to the top of *Holm Hill* on opening day. *Towards the south we see right across the border into Bewcastle and Nicholforest, the Cumberland hills forming a most effective background, while the view to the north is equally extensive.*

Bewcastle is easy to pass by, and given the proximity of the 'b' and the 'n' on the QWERTY keyboard could be easily dismissed as a typo. Peter Davidson, in *The Idea of North*, describes it as *the last of England* or, from the perspective of *Holm Hill*, the first. The sheep and cattle roam free under the Borders' wide skies, at a point where Northumberland, Cumbria and southernmost Scotland meet.

And yet, for all its remoteness, there is evidence that at various times in ancient history this place possessed real significance. There is a corvid-haunted castle, the church which stands on the same land once occupied by a Roman fort, and within the graveyard the Bewcastle Cross, the finest Anglo-Saxon cross in Europe, dating from the seventh century.

Peter Davidson, again in *The Idea of North*, says *this is as sophisticated an artefact as the England of the late seventh century was capable of producing; it has details consonant with the sculpture of contemporary Rome. It forces a reconsideration of the whole question of centre and periphery, standing as it now does in a hamlet at the very edge of England, where to go further north you would have to walk to reach Scotland. By drove roads, moss-troopers' tracks and memorised secret paths to the frontier.*

Moss troopers, brigands from the mid seventeenth century and the Reivers for centuries before, this Debatable and Border Land was forever unquiet. Hardly on the edge of events, it was at the very heart of a war zone, and much of it is visible from *Holm Hill*.

The par 4 fourth, *On the Flat*, plays out across the top of the course, on the level, as the name implies—a welcome relief after the steady ascent up the first three holes. Although the course had always been rented from the Buccleuch Estates, it has recently

211

transferred into the ownership of a village trust. This transfer of ownership has been the catalyst for ambitious plans to build a new clubhouse and holiday accommodation at the top of the course with improved vehicular access. This would be a stunning location for the nineteenth hole, and it must be hoped the plans come to fruition. Presumably, this would lead to a change in the sequence of holes, but until then the fourth is followed by the downhill par 3, *Cow Hill*, named after the nearby herd of cows which can be regularly seen in the adjacent field and occasionally on the course, despite being fenced since 1979. These are animals with a sense of history.

To the rear of the fifth green is the fifteenth tee box, but from the sixth tee, *Quarry*, is more than 60 yards shorter. The fairway descends some 40 feet, with the green offset to the left. The putting surface slopes to the rear, such that an approach shot must be pitched short. It is deceptively difficult to finish with a tidy score. The shorter par 4 seventh, *Hawthorns*, is to the left and plays back up the hill, at which point Newcastleton delivers a sting in the tail.

The par 4 eighth tee, *Lakeland Hills*, is positioned about halfway back down the seventh fairway, through the trees to the left. For the uninitiated it can be difficult to find. That mild frustration is nothing when compared to the potential disaster that awaits at these last two holes. Both severe dog-legs, it is only right and proper that they come in pairs. The eighth demands a decent drive positioned left on the fairway. Even in the ideal position, the second shot is to a green more than 50 feet above, with only the top of the pin just visible—difficult enough, but go right, and even this vague directional clue disappears amid hawthorns and heavy rough. A card-destroying hole if you get it wrong; a delight to get right, I imagine.

The second dog-leg, *Stone Hole*, completes the round. The green is out of sight, adjacent to the equally invisible clubhouse. A par 4 on the front nine at 452 yards and a par 5 on the back at 512 yards—that extra shot comes in very handy and adjusts the stroke index from 4 to 9. Descending around 120 feet, the sharp turn 300 yards down the fairway demands an exceptional drive. Ordinary mortals coming up short can elect to pitch to the corner and hope for a third landing near the pin. The alternative is to cut the corner, playing blind over heavy rough and trees. It is a glorious finish on a par with the final hole at Killin. Hidden on lesser-known, out-of-the-way courses are some of the best golf holes you will find anywhere.

After the ups and downs of the Newcastleton course, it must have been some relief that the walk to the station was all downhill. Today there is little evidence that the railway ever existed, and yet it was once a vital part of this small, out-of-the-way community.

The level crossings that once intersected Langholm Street are long gone, but they would play a significant part in the history of the Waverley Line as it faced its final curtain. As that last Night Midland service to St Pancras approached Newcastleton, the Peak Class diesel, D60 *Lytham St Annes*, was faced with a red light. The level-crossing gates were closed against the express service as the parish minister and a crowd in excess of 200 villagers formed a human barrier. The local constabulary arrested the minister, the Rev. Brydon Mabon, but his flock refused to budge. It was long gone midnight, and tempers were frayed.

Raised from his sleeping compartment, it was Liberal MP for Selkirk, Roxburgh and Peebles, David Steel, who was obliged to dismount the train and negotiate a settlement. In return for the release of the minister, the crowd agreed to let the train proceed. In a scene reminiscent of an Ealing comedy, the Rev. Mabon, to show there were no hard feelings, would invite all seventeen police officers involved in the protest to tea at the manse. He had campaigned for three years to save the line, but the battle was lost. *The reason for the demonstration was that we now feel cut off, but any further protest seems pointless. The line is shut.*[7]

It was a short train ride from Newcastleton back to Riccarton Junction via Steele Road and the connection with the Border Counties Line to Hexham.[8] Another regular on this line was the V2 60955 out of St Margaret's shed, Edinburgh. It is this hard-worked engine I imagine climbing the gradient out of Newcastleton and easing into Riccarton Junction, a single-carriage Hexham train waiting in the Border Counties Railway (BCR) southern bay at the end of the station buildings.

It is quite possibly a Class J21 0-6-0, introduced in 1886 and still operating in the 1950s—65061 was a regular sight on the BCR. Walk out to lonely Riccarton today, and almost all evidence of its former glories has been erased. It is near impossible to imagine this was once a thriving railway centre. *A village of thirty-seven houses was built for the railway workers and their families, together with a school and mission hall. The station buildings contained a branch of Hawick Co-op and a post office. Church services were held in the waiting room, the minister reaching the station by walking along the railway from Saughtree. Burials were not conducted at Riccarton; coffins were conveyed to Newcastleton, where interment took place.*[9]

It is a scene from Dickens. A lone figure, stovepipe hat and black clad, tramping the snow-covered line through the dead of a winter's night to offer solace to the dying at the junction. Over 2 miles and a near 300-foot climb around Shiel Knowe, how often was snow kicked from boots at the midnight door, but kicked too late?

We can put a name to at least one of these ministers. The 1881 census lists the Saughtree Station agent as James Unwin, who lived in the station buildings with his wife and son of four months. James was also the preacher.[10]

Leaving Saughtree, the BCR crossed the Dawstonburn Viaduct (now demolished), maintaining the high ground above Liddell Water before arcing south, crossing the border and calling at the first station in England, Deadwater. I am all but home. In 1932 a *Daily Mirror* reporter applied some artistic licence, claiming that the tiny platform was half in Scotland, half in England. To be pedantic, the actual border is about 100 yards north, where it follows the path of Deadwater Rigg in a culvert under the railway line. This was once marked by a large and ornate Scotland–England sign, the Scottish side marked by a thistle and the English side by a rose. When the line was closed, the sign was rescued and now resides in the National Railway Museum at York.

The national newspaper took an interest in Deadwater because it was deemed a *place of distinction*. Since the early 1900s the station had been operated by women, and the resident station-mistress in 1932 was Miss Margaret Wylie, who also acted as shunter, lamp woman and, on rare occasions, ticket collector. *Her day is long, for she has to be on duty when the first train reaches Deadwater at 06:51, and she must see the last train off at*

215

17:13. The most important part of her work is with goods trains. She is often called upon to shunt, and to efficiently shunt means that her work includes the greasing of points. Her station is lit by oil lamps which have to have daily attention.[11] Margaret lived alone in splendid isolation, with just a few hens for company and not even a radio. It is a desolate enough spot in the twenty-first century, but in the early twentieth century Deadwater, its station and its well must have seemed like the world's end. At the edge of civilisation, Miss Wylie sleeps, and *moves from England to Scotland whenever she walks from one room to another.* You must admire the reporter's invention.

To the north of Deadwater is the stern and dark-hued Peel Fell, the source of both the North Tyne and Liddell Water. A series of burns, including Deadwater and Bells, feed into the North Tyne just above Kerseycleugh Bridge. At Kielder Castle it joins Kielder Burn and becomes a serious stretch of water. The BCR keeps close with the North Tyne for much of its length to Hexham.

Just south of the castle, the BCR flies the North Tyne on the Kielder Viaduct. It is a magnificent example of a skew-arch construction which demanded that each stone in the arches should be individually shaped in accordance with the system established by Peter Nicholson of Newcastle-upon-Tyne, a pioneer geo-metrician. To the soundtrack of steam and clacking wheels, the train would rock and roll along this empty valley, passing through Lewiefield Halt, Plashetts and the Colliery Waggonway before reaching Falstone. Walk along the old line today, and about a mile south of the viaduct, the old track bed disappears beneath Kielder Water Reservoir. Officially opened by Queen Elizabeth II on the 26 May 1982, it is the diminutive burns springing from Peel Fell which feed this 170-foot-deep, 44-billion-gallon, man-made lake.

Evidence of the BCR does not fully reappear until south of Kielder Dam, just north of Falstone. Much else lies beneath the reservoir: Lewiefield Halt, Plashetts Colliery, the station, parts of the old village, various farms and HMS *Standard*. Sadly, a prolonged drought will not reveal ghost villages, as the buildings were destroyed before the valley was flooded. Nor will the superstructure of some long-lost battleship emerge—HMS *Standard* was a shore-based assessment and rehabilitation centre for naval personnel diagnosed with personality disorders. Whatever inspired the reservoir's civil engineers, it wasn't the Lost City of Atlantis.

Keeping to the high ground above the Tyne, the line tracks ever southward, through the level crossing at Thorneyburn, over another skewed-arch viaduct, Knoppingholme, just north of Tarset Station, through long-abandoned Charlton Station, arriving next at Bellingham. Easing under the road bridge that carries the B6320 from Otterburn to the town centre, the livestock auction mart was to the right, closed in 2004, and on the left is Bellingham Golf Club, established in 1893.

Despite being closed for more than fifty years, evidence of the BCR can be found everywhere. The stone-built Bellingham Station survives in its original form, as do many of the stations heading south to Hexham—Wark, Barrasford, Chollerton, Humshaugh and Wall are all still standing. Almost all are now desirable private residences—at Bellingham and Wall there are even British Railways Mk 1 carriages to fire the imagination of the nostalgic.[12] The modern-day desirability of these buildings has much to do with their location, which points to a more fundamental truth: they are, for the most part, in entirely the wrong place for the communities they served. Wark is a prime example.

A moderately sized village, the station is on the wrong side of the river, nearly a mile distant from the centre and up the steep hill to Comogan. Geography played its part, but wealthy nimbyism along the North Tyne Valley was also responsible. *The landowners and the big house owners, they all objected to the smoke of the steam engines. Then, when the combustion engine came along, the railways were remote from the villages, and naturally the people could get the bus rather having to walk the mile or mile and a half to the railway station. And this was the downfall of the rural district line.*[13]

One and a half miles south of Wall Station, the South Tyne and the North Tyne meet before the line crossed the combined waters to the west of Hexham. The footings of the bridge still stand, well proud of the river. On Thursday, 12 August 1948, after unprecedented rainfall, two masonry spans were damaged by the fast-running Tyne. A temporary repair was put in place and stayed there, with an associated 10 mph speed restriction, until the last passenger service crossed the bridge on 13 October 1956. As early as 1948, the newly nationalised railways were reluctant to invest in the BCR. The writing was on the wall. The BCR ended at the junction on the southern side of the Tyne, where it connected with the Newcastle and Carlisle Railways before arriving a few minutes later into Hexham. According to the July 1922 *Bradshaw Railway Guide*, a train departing Newcastleton at 09:01 would arrive at Riccarton Junction at 09:23. A connecting service to Hexham departed at 10:02, arriving at 11:43. It was then over two hours before the Allendale train departed at 14:15. The passenger service was quite possibly pulled by an LNER Class F8, built at Gateshead works between 1886 and 1892. The steam engine numbered 423 was a regular on the run to Allendale and remained in service until 1933. This side-tank engine would travel briefly along the

Newcastle to Carlisle Line before branching left a few hundred yards beyond the junction with the BCR.

A short stretch of the line has disappeared beneath the A69, but much of its original 12-mile track bed can still be traced as it takes a circuitous route via Elrington, Langley and Staward before terminating at Catton Road at 14:48. Like the BCR stations, the end of the line at Allendale was an inconvenient one mile distant from the town centre. The original Railway Act presented to Parliament proposed terminating the line at Path Foot in Allendale, with a potential extension to Allenheads, but none of this came to fruition. Conveniently, the Allendale Golf Club at Thornley Gate, which transferred to High Studdon in 1998, was less than a half-mile walk from the station. Quite by chance, and as if to prove the interdependence of golf and rail, the two gentlemen in the foreground of this image are carrying golf clubs.

THE RAILWAY STATION, ALLENDALE. 2186.

I imagine … I have arrived late in the season and late in the day. The sun is low, and the smoke from 100 chimney pots hangs in the still air above the dale. The year is hurrying down towards the short days as a I walk up the hill to Thornley Gate. It's not dark yet, but it's getting there.

> *In midnights of November,*
> *When Dead Man's Fair is nigh,*
> *And danger in the valley,*
> *And anger in the sky,*
>
> *Around the huddling homesteads,*
> *The leafless timber roars,*
> *And the dead call the dying,*
> *And finger at the doors.*[14]

The lights are on in the Ashleigh Hotel, casting a glow across the first and seventh tees to the side of the small clubhouse. There is time enough for nine holes. Green fee in the honesty box, a ticket tied to the carry bag and a scorecard in my back pocket, it is an uphill par 3 for openers.

The Thornley Gate course is tough; if you cannot hit a straight ball, you are in trouble. Cattle roam free on the course, and the greens are protected by electrified fencing which packs a punch. The fairways are cut to exactly a chain's width, 22 yards. The cattle do not distinguish between fairway and semi-rough. Cowpats, which litter the fairway, are assiduously shovelled to the side, such that this extra-fertilised pasture thrives. Finding a ball that strays into this stuff is a lottery.

The greens are built square, mostly elevated and the same size—about fourteen paces. There are necessary local rules about electrified fence posts and cowpats:

> *When a ball which has been played within 20 yards of the posts or wires surrounding a green strikes the posts or wires, the ball may be lifted, without penalty, and dropped as near to the place as possible from which it was originally played, but not nearer to the hole.*

> *A ball lying in dung may be lifted and dropped not nearer to and in line with the hole without penalty.*

When a ball lies in a rabbit scrape or definite hoof mark on the fairway, it may be lifted and dropped not nearer to the hole without penalty.

The scope for interpretation and discussion about *20 yards from the hole*, *lying in dung* and a *definite hoof mark* is infinite.

Trees left and right form a broad avenue to the first green. This sense of enclosure disappears between the second and fifth as the course takes to the higher ground. The second tee is some 100 yards north, adjacent to the road that leads up the old quarries at Cleugh Head and to High Broadwood Hall, the original location of Allendale Golf Club, established in 1906 and closed during the Great War. A letter to the *Newcastle Journal*'s sporting editor in October 1917 explains the predicament:

Sir,

Golfers accustomed to visit Allendale and its picturesque 18-hole course will hear with regret that the club, owing to the war, cannot continue the tenancy, and the cost of making it [sic]—over £200—will be lost. I would like to know if the committee have personally approached the landlord, because many of the golfers think that he is a gentleman who would certainly not allow the course to go down while its principal supporters are abroad fighting for us.

It would be a great disappointment to many on their return to find the golf course gone. Besides, it is the leading attraction to a large number of people who visit Allendale.

Yours, etc.

JW

Presumably, the landlord did not quite live up to his gentlemanly reputation. This image shows the 1906 opening ceremony at High Broadwood Hall.[15]

The second hole is perhaps the hardest on the course—uphill into a prevailing wind, with out-of-bounds all the way up the right, a sliced ball into the farm can ruin a card too early in the round. To the side of the fairway is one of the 2-mile-long smelting flues that run up from Allen Mill to the chimneys on Flow Moss. It was in one of these flues, in 1931, that greenkeeper Fred Stobart was found dead, with a wound to his throat and a blood-stained razor in his right hand. A verdict of 'suicide while of unsound mind' was returned at the inquest. It can be a lonely job at the best of times, and not best suited to someone with suicidal tendencies. Perhaps golfers, too ready to blame the course for their poor play, should be a little less willing to air their grievances.

Survive the second, and the par 3 across the top of the course comes as some relief. The shadows are lengthening and High Studdon is illuminated across the valley—it would make a fine alternative location for the golf course. In the meantime, the fourth and fifth, both par 4s, play north-east down the course and then back up again to the testing sixth, a long downhill par 4. From an elevated tee, it is a glorious drive, but the longer the drive, the greater any deviation in flight is amplified. It is not uncommon to lose half a dozen balls in a single round—cattle must rattle to the sound of undigested Dunlops.

The par 4 seventh plays uphill from a tee adjacent to the clubhouse, emitting a yellow-green light against the dim afternoon.

A steep approach to an elevated green, the pin can be difficult to see against the setting sun. The race is on to complete the round before dark. The course has no bunkers, and no ditches or ponds; the narrow fairways and challenging semi are deemed hard enough. Just now and then, the course may respond to skill or good fortune; it depends on your point of view.

A Thornley Gate golfing story:

Two brothers are standing at the par 3 eighth tee on a rain-sodden afternoon. The younger sibling, only just tolerated by the older, takes the 8-iron from his bag and lines up for the green. The sweetly struck ball climbs high in the air from the elevated tee and lands with a splash right next to the pin. "That might be in!" exclaims the excited youngster.

"Is it fuck!" replies his older brother.

Nevertheless, it was. In a repeat of the Tony Jacklin hole-in-one conversation (Chapter 4), the elder brother asked which club his young brother had used. "An 8-iron? That's far too much club. I use a pitching wedge!"

My 9-iron gets nowhere near repeating the trick.

As I approach the last, my bag feels lighter. The number of balls I am carrying has shrunk, at least two sleeves lost to the too-lush semi-rough. Every story, taken to its logical conclusion, is about loss. My twenty-year golfing 'career' hit the heights in 2013 with a string of trophies and medals. Since then it has been a slow decline. There has been the occasional renaissance, but the unerring handicap trend has been northwards.

My life philosophy is to disregard decline, but some things are difficult to ignore. My dad was already gone when I started this journey, but my mum was still clinging to the wreckage—she passed over somewhere between Traigh and Lochcarron.

And then, tragically, my big sister joined them between Cullen and Carrbridge. I am all that remains to remember who we once were.

The last is a downhill par 4, with the road to Carrshield and out-of-bounds to the right. It is reachable in one by those of a certain skill level and physical disposition. So, allow me this final luxury. A long drive, straight down the middle, leaving a short pitch to the green. In the dim light I lose sight of the ball, but you always know when you have struck one sweet and true. I cannot spin the ball by design, so my pitch lands short and runs on a few yards to within feet of the pin. Standing over the birdie-putt, the twilight is enhanced by the yellow light shining through the clubhouse windows. I am distracted by the shadowy outline of three figures gathered in the centre of the room and miss the simple putt. A man in his late twenties, wearing a heavy tweed suit, an elbow on the table, a cigarette raised to his face. Smoke obscures their features. The woman, in a utility dress, is deep in conversation, forever breaking the silence, while a small girl with a serious expression looks on earnestly. I should cross over and join them, but not just yet. I am going home. I have no idea what happens next.

Notes

1.   The lyrics for 'Going Home' are written to accompany Dvorak's famous 'Largo' theme from his 'New World Symphony'. The symphony was first performed by the New York Philharmonic at Carnegie Hall on 16 December 1893. This was one of the pieces of music which accompanied the *Apollo 11* mission to the moon. The lyrics were written by one of Dvorak's pupils, William Arms Fisher (1861–1948).

2.   For those continuing by road (there is no other option), turn left out of the golf course and follow the B6359 as far as Hawick. From there, follow the B6399 until its junction with the B6357, turn right over the narrow river-bridge, and Newcastleton is 2 miles further south. At the end of the green space (Douglas Square) in the centre of the town, turn right into Langholm Street, and the golf course is approximately a half a mile distant, on high ground overlooking the valley. These roads approximately follow the route of the Waverley Line. On the B6399, significant sections are visible nearby, including Shankend Viaduct and Whitrope Siding, now the site of the Whitrope Heritage Centre, just south of the tunnel (closed due to partial collapse).

3.   Chapter 4, 'The Waverley Route: Out with a Bang', *Forgotten Railways Scotland*, John Thomas.

4.   Information supplied by the Stobs Military Camp website: http://www.stobscamp.org.

5.   A poem by Joseph Bramwell Bush of the RAMC, supplied by Stobs Military Camp (1903–1959), http://stobs-camp.bizhat.com.

6.   *A Hundred Years On: A history of the Newcastleton Club* by Fred Ewart, published in the year of its centenary, 1994.

7.   *Newcastle Journal*, Tuesday, 7 January 1969, 'Tea at the Manse After Rail Blockade'.

8.   The route by road to Hexham is 8 miles north out of Newcastleton, following the B6357 as far as the Saughtree junction where, Kielder Water is

signposted *9 miles*. Follow this road 24 miles south until you reach the Riverdale Hall Hotel. At the T-junction just beyond, turn right onto the B6320 and drive the 12 miles to Chollerford. Cross the Tyne at the traffic-light-controlled bridge, and then turn right onto the A6079 through Wall and Acomb until you reach the A69 junction. Turn left and then first right off the dual carriageway into Hexham. The railway station is to the left of the second bridge. The journey from Hexham to Allendale is described in the first book, in reverse.

9. 'North British Railway Lines: Border Counties Railway', *Railways in Northumberland*, Alan Young.

10. From 'The Story of Saughtree Railway Station – 1892 to the present day', Geoff Mann, October 2018. Geoff is the current owner of the station, the preserved line and operational Ruston diesel shunter 275882 (*Meg of Saughtree*).

11. 'Woman Runs a Station: Railway Outpost in Two Countries', *Daily Mirror*, Saturday, 16 April 1932.

12. At Bellingham there are a pair of Mk 1 railway carriages. Sitting on rails outside the station building, they operate as Carriages Tea Room. The single carriage at Wall was once used as a café but is now closed.

13. A BCR engine driver talking in the 1986 Coast to Coast documentary, *Slow Train to Riccarton*.

14. From A. E. Housman's *Last Poems* (1922) XIX: *I publish these poems, few though they are, because it is not likely that I shall ever be impelled to write much more. I can no longer expect to be revisited by the continuous excitement under which in the early months of 1895 I wrote the greater part of my first book, nor indeed could I well sustain it if it came.*

15. The image was kindly supplied by Scott Keenleyside, a golf professional at Highland Pacific golf course, Victoria, British Columbia, Canada. Scott's father's family originates from Allendale.

Bibliography

Baker, R., (2015), *Beautiful Idiots and Brilliant Lunatics*, Amberley Books, Stroud, Gloucestershire

Berger, J., (1992), *Keeping a Rendezvous*, Granta Books, London

Boyd, J., (2006), *White Bicycles – Making Music in the 1960s*, Serpent's Tail

Campbell, V., (2008), *Camp 165 Watten*, Whittles Publishing

Carruthers, B., (2011), *Wolf Pack: The U-Boats at War*, Pen & Sword Maritime Books

Connolly, R., (1981), *John Lennon 1940–1980*, Fontana Paperbacks

Davidson, P., (2005), *The Idea of North*, Reaktion Books Limited

Dore, R. N., (1972), *A History of Hale, Cheshire: From Domesday to Dormitory*, John Sherratt and Son Ltd, Altrincham

Dunn, D. R., (2014), *Steam Memories: 1950's–1960's The Border Counties Railway Parts 1 and 2*, Book Law Publications, Nottingham

Elton, G., 1st Baron Elton (1939), *The Life of Ramsay MacDonald*. Collins, London

Ewart, F., (1974), *A Hundred Years On (Newcastleton Golf Club 1894–1994)*, Eskdale Print (Scotland)

Gordon, B., (2004), *Bonar Bridge, Ardgay Golf Club: A Celebration of 100 years of Community Golf*, Local Press

Griffiths, J., (2006), *Wild: An Elemental Journey*, Penguin Group (USA)

Hendrick, B., (1932), *The Life of Andrew Carnegie*. Doubleday, Doran & Co., New York

Hendrick, B. and Henderson, D., (1950), *Louise Whitfield Carnegie: The Life of Mrs. Andrew Carnegie*, Hastings House, New York

Houghton, G., (1958), *Golf on my Pillow*, Stanley Paul & Co. Ltd., London

Hubert Walker, J., (1948), *On Hills of the North*, Oliver and Boyd

Janes, D., (2017), *Death at Wolf's Nick: The Killing of Evelyn Foster*, Mirror Books

Lawrence, K., (2005), *John Lennon: In his Own Words*, Andrews McMeel Publishing

Macpherson, S., (2015), *Golf's Royal Clubs: Honoured by The British Royal Family 1833–2013*, The Royal & Ancient, St Andrews

Martin-Jenkins, C., (2012), *CMJ: A Cricketing Life*. Simon & Schuster UK Ltd.

McGhee, N., (2003), *Killermont: The Home of Glasgow Golf Club*, Glasgow Golf Club

Nasaw, D., (2006), *Andrew Carnegie*, The Penguin Press, New York

Penrose, L., (2006), *Reay Golf Club: A Guide to the Environmental and Conservation Management at Reay Golf Course*, ParSaver Golf

Pottinger, G., (1972), *Muirfield and the Honourable Company*, Scottish Academic Press

Ratcliffe Barnett, T., (1930), *Autumns in Skye, Ross and Sutherland*, Simpkin Marshall Ltd.

Ridley, J., (2012), *Bertie: A Life of Edward VII*, Chatto & Windus, London

Stedman, M. L., (2012), *The Light Between Oceans*, Transworld Publishers, London

Sutherland, J., (2016), *Golf Causerie: John Sutherland of Royal Dornoch Golf Club*, Robin K. Bargmann, The Netherlands

Thomas, J., (1976), *Forgotten Railways: Scotland*, David & Charles, Newton Abbot, Devon

Winterson, J., (2011), *Why Be Happy When You Could Be Normal?*, Jonathan Cape, Random House, London

Young, A., (2003), *Railways in Northumberland*, Amadeus Press, Cleckheaton, West Yorkshire

Appendix 1

I hear the voice of the restless sea
I must answer its age-old call;
And I must climb old Sandside Head
'Ere the gloaming shadows fall.

Up by old 'Ned' and dark Goe Grant
By the track on the oft-climbed steep;
Till I saw the sun in his fiery robes
Sweep down to the far-flung deep.

When the old, grey cliffs are rosy bright
In the ruddy sunset glow,
And the fulmars wheel on wings of fire,
As they shuttle to and fro.

Here the day's cares cease and the heart finds peace,
'Tis sufficient that I am here;
But I still may think of the days gone by,
And the loved ones of yesteryear.

How oft did they come to this self-same spot,
At the close of a summer's day,
Who are now laid in a dreamless sleep
In the churchyard across the bay.

Still the restless tides sweep to and fro,
On the 'Scarf Rock' breaks the surf;
In a mist of blue the scillas blow
Above the wind-shorn surf.

The familiar hills like guardians stand,
Round the same old, dear old Reay,
And the crescent sands like a golden band,
Still enclasps the sapphire bay.

But those who trod the Head's green sod,
They breast the steep no more;
The day's toil past; the boat made fast;
And silent lies the oar.

But here shall I come while the sands shall run,
And life's short span shall last;
For 'tis ever here that I shall feel them near,
Seafarers of the past.

And when the last sun sets for me,
And I sail for the 'Other Side'
I shall see them stand on as fair a strand,
And their outstretched hands shall guide.

When I've steered my course o'er that unknown sea
By the twin stars—Faith and Hope,
At their well-known hail, I shall furl my sail;
And they'll pass me my mooring rope.

Robert S. Stephen